ABANDONED VERMONT AND NEW HAMPSHIRE

FORGOTTEN IN THE MOUNTAINS

MARIE DESROSIERS

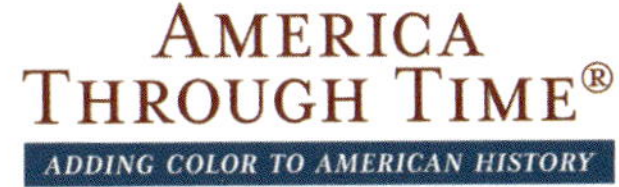

America Through Time is an imprint of Fonthill Media LLC
www.through-time.com
office@through-time.com

Published by Arcadia Publishing by arrangement with Fonthill Media LLC
For all general information, please contact Arcadia Publishing:
Telephone: 843-853-2070
Fax: 843-853-0044
E-mail: sales@arcadiapublishing.com
For customer service and orders:
Toll-Free 1-888-313-2665

www.arcadiapublishing.com

First published 2023

ISBN 978-1-63499-455-2

Typeset in Trade Gothic 10pt on 15pt
Printed and bound in England

CONTENTS

ABOUT THE AUTHOR

MARIE DESROSIERS is a hobby photographer with a love and fascination for the forgotten and abandoned. Whenever possible, she seeks to find the history and stories behind the places she comes across. Marie spends much of her time driving down backroads to find the often-overlooked beauty and lost history in these abandoned homes, farms, and businesses. Where others may see crumbling structures, she finds unappreciated beauty that she documents in her photographs. She has a passion and determination to capture these places before nature reclaims them. She is hopeful that through these photos, these places can be truly seen and remembered, even briefly.

INTRODUCTION

If there's something I've learned over the past couple of years since the start and completion of my first book, *Abandoned Vermont: Down Forgotten Backroads,* it's that things can, and often do, change much faster than you may be prepared for. Looking back on that book and looking at the photos of places that are no longer standing, whether due to nature or human-caused reasons, makes me grateful that I was able to at least memorialize them through photography. When I'm photographing these structures, I very frequently think about the fact that despite people and time eventually moving on and forgetting, nature doesn't forget. It creeps in through the doors falling off their hinges, the broken, dirty windows, the cracks and holes in the floorboards, and it reclaims the spaces that belonged to it in the first place. It shakes the foundations and reminds you that it's there, and that it's a force to be reckoned with.

In the summer of 2021, I spent a great deal of my time not only regaining my strength from an unexpected transplant in February, but also reminding myself that time is fleeting, and I should spend it doing the things that I enjoy. There are few things that I enjoy more than grabbing my camera, getting in my car with no real destination in mind, putting on music, and driving until I find the things that others have forgotten. I was, and still am, grateful to still have this opportunity, and am hopeful that I'll still have many more days of being able to do what I love. I couldn't do this if not for the people who stepped in to literally save my life, in numerous ways. I'm thankful for my partner, Scott, my family, my dog, Sukha, who got me through my hardest days, my friends, my medical team, and my selfless donor and their family who have given me the irreplaceable gift of more time.

Abandoned Vermont and New Hampshire: Forgotten in the Mountains

On winding dirt roads, with beautiful backdrops of mountains and thick forests, forgotten treasures hide tucked away, waiting to be remembered. In the most rural of these mountain towns, some of these places and memories have been abandoned for years. From small camps and cabins, which have long since seen their last hunting season, to large farmhouses with fields overgrown and choked with weeds, this type of abandonment is often overlooked, because it's not as sought out, visible, or as flashy as the derelict spaces in larger, more populated areas. What rural abandonment lacks in its "showiness," it typically makes up for in deep-rooted familial and local history. When driving around these mountain towns, through backroads that connect you from one small town to the next, and looking at the rural abandonment, you gain a respect for the ability of these places to withstand years of harsh winters and the toll nature can take when something becomes forgotten. These abandoned places sit empty, like fading reminders of the promised American dream.

1

RESPECTING THE LAND

On a cool, crisp October morning, a friend and I set out to find the folkloric Brunswick Springs. We parked my car and walked down the very quiet dirt road. The only noises we heard were coming from the crunching of the amber-colored maple leaves beneath our feet that had been falling from the branches overhead, to the dismay of those who had come to the area for leaf-peeping. These springs, once called "The Eighth Wonder of the World" by Ripley's Believe It or Not, are found in the woods, in a remote corner of Vermont. The Abenaki, who are native to this area, rely on the healing powers of the water and consider the land to be sacred. The six individual springs all contain a different mineral—calcium, magnesium, sulfur, bromide, arsenic, and iron. They all flow from under a steep hill and merge together, before running into the river below. As the story goes, in 1748, a soldier who had been injured and brought by companions to the springs had become healed by the water. When he returned and tried to bottle and profit from the water, a struggle ensued, and an Abenaki baby and man were killed. The understandably distraught mother of the baby, an Abenaki woman, placed a curse on the springs, and it was said that anyone who tried to profit from them would fail.

As with many places like this (such as the Elgin Springs House, which I wrote about in my last book), word spread and soon people began to flock to the area in hopes of taking, and sometimes selling, the healing water. With the influx of people came the first house to be built just above the springs in 1832. Later, in 1860, a hotel called the Brunswick Springs House was built, where it operated for several years. The views from the hotel, which sat at the top of the hill, were of the Connecticut River as well as the White Mountains of New Hampshire. According to a hotel brochure, there were sixty guest chambers where the "medicine waters" were piped in. The hotel was enlarged in 1894 and then, almost immediately, it burned down. The owner, Dr. Rowell, rebuilt the hotel, which he named Pine Crest Lodge, shortly after the turn of the century, right before his passing. The Pine Crest Lodge was then taken over by John Hutchins and burned down in 1929. Hutchins decided to have two more hotels built in 1930 and 1931, but as with the others, they burned to the ground. Combustion of paint fumes was shown to be the cause of one of the fires, but the cause of the others remains undetermined. Eventually, people stopped building on the land they had exploited for so long.

The springs still exist and are still considered sacred by the Abenaki. People continue to go there and leave tokens of appreciation at the springs. The final hotel foundations and staircases, though covered in vines and overgrowth, are still visible and serve as a reminder that sacred land should be treated with respect, as should the people who it belongs to.

There have been a few tragedies on the land, and people who live near the springs do talk about a "strange feeling" that can be felt in the area. Though I didn't necessary feel anything that caused me any kind of discomfort there, I was in awe of the beauty and stillness.

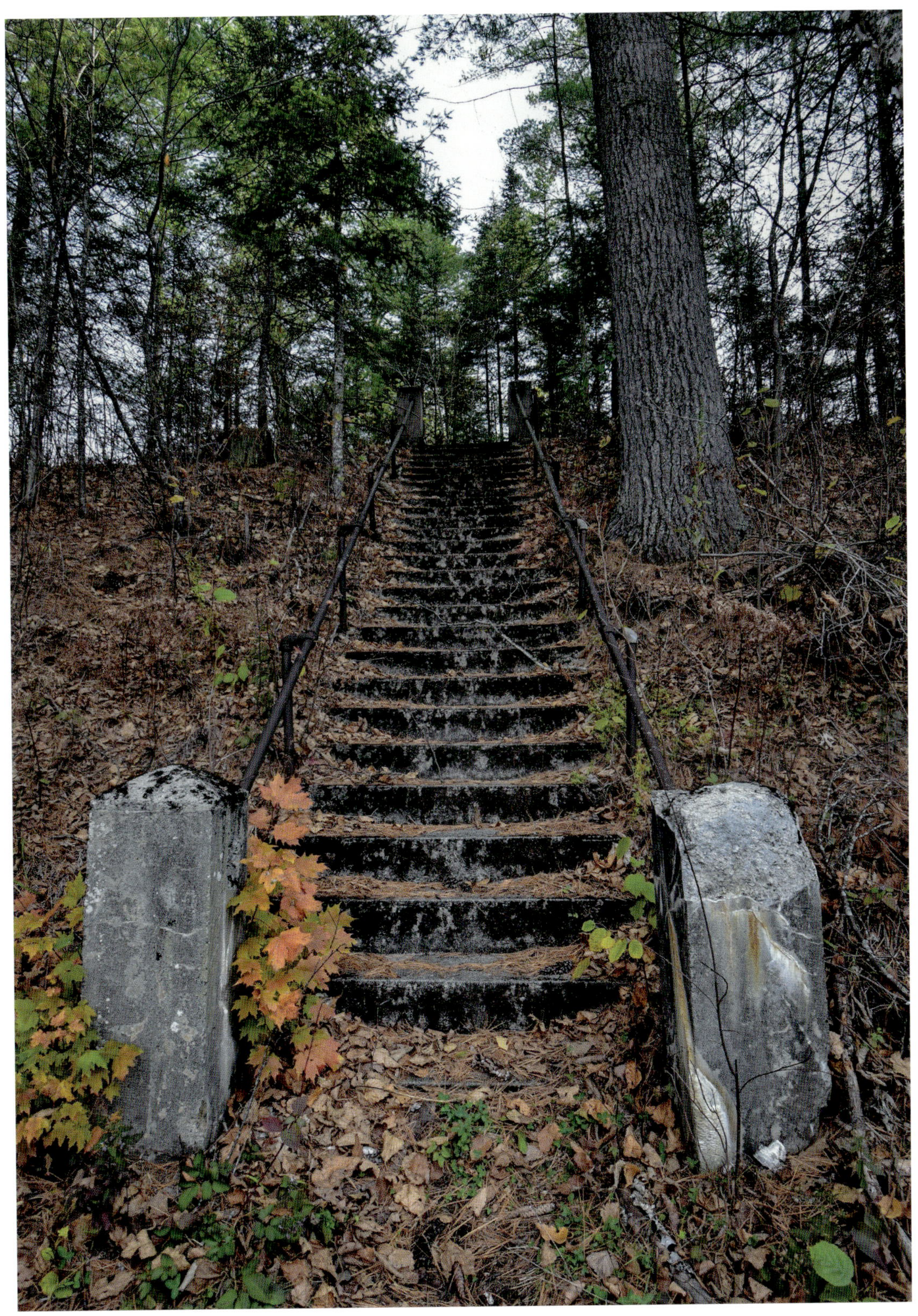

Staircase leading to the top of the springs.

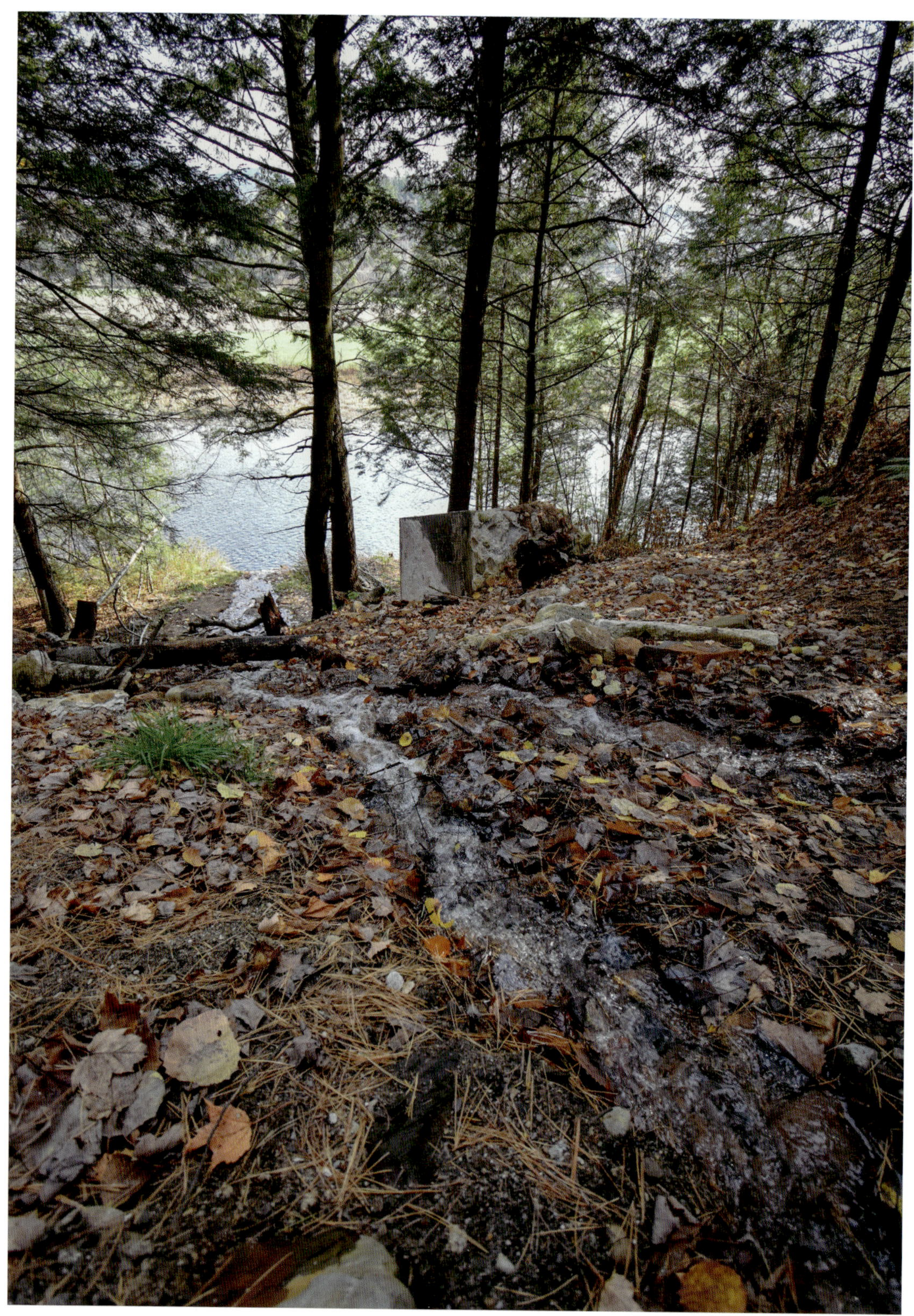

The six springs merging and running into the river below.

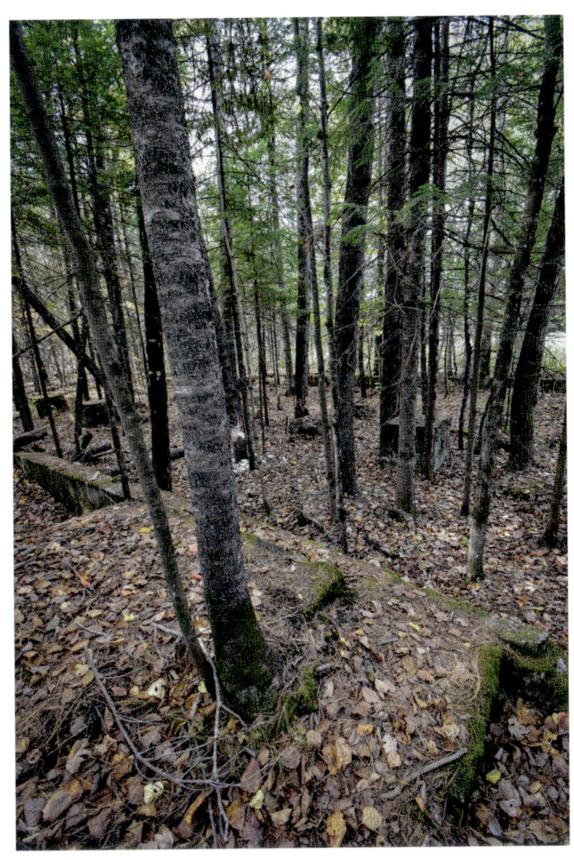

Foundations of the last hotel to be built on the land.

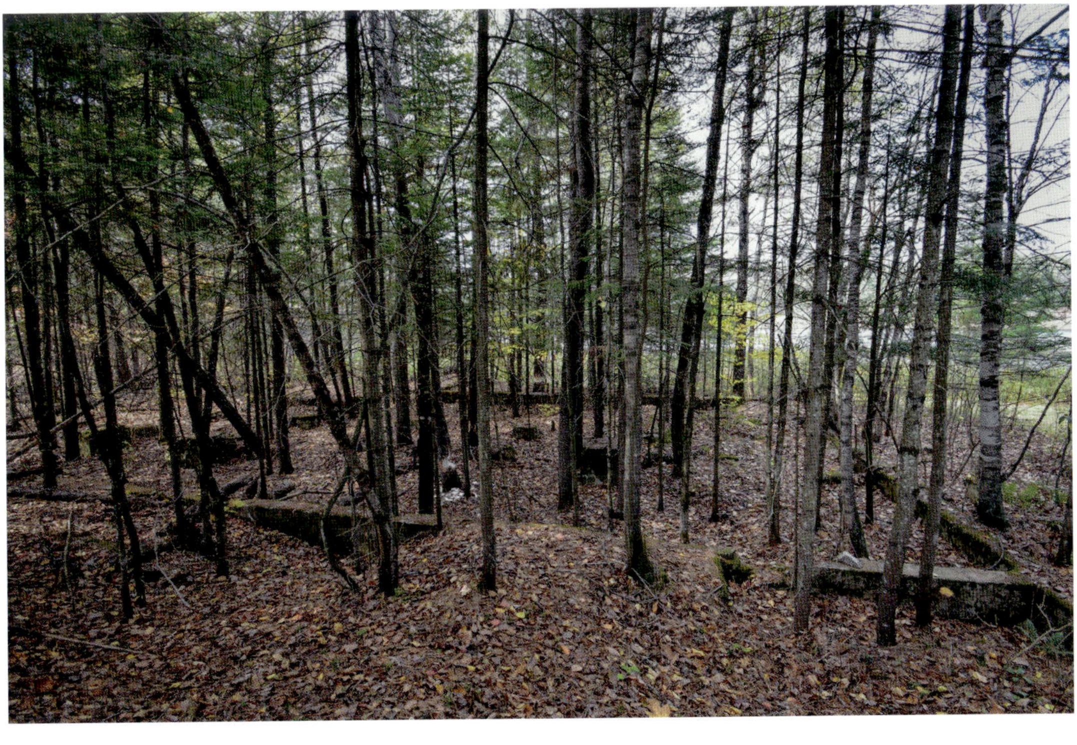

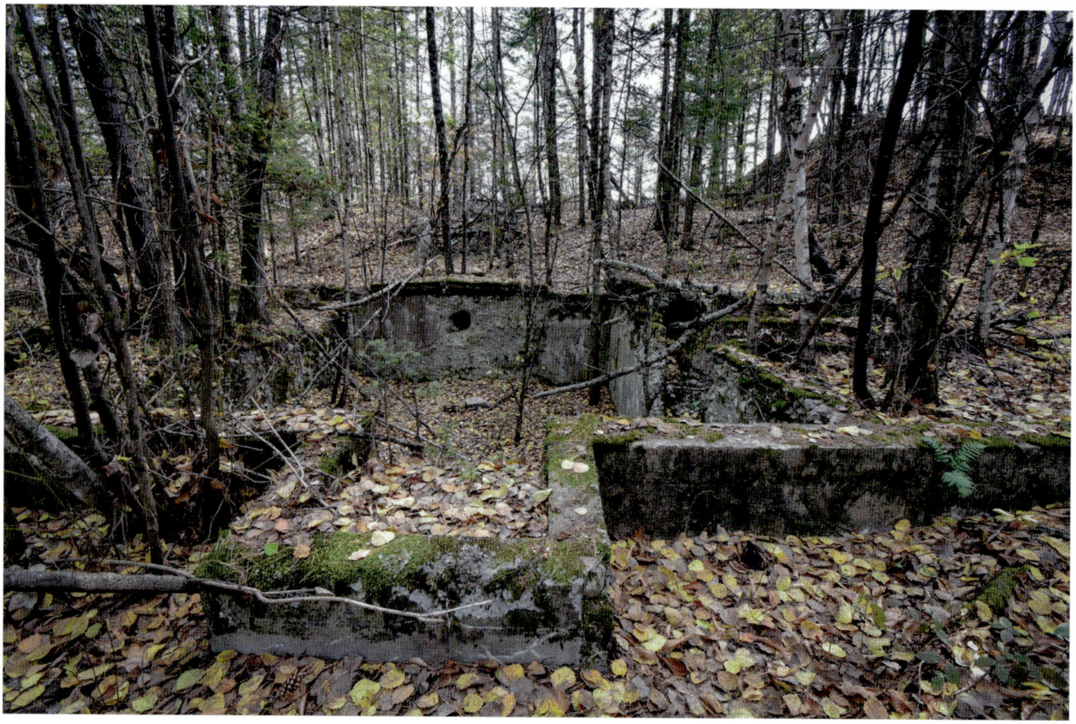

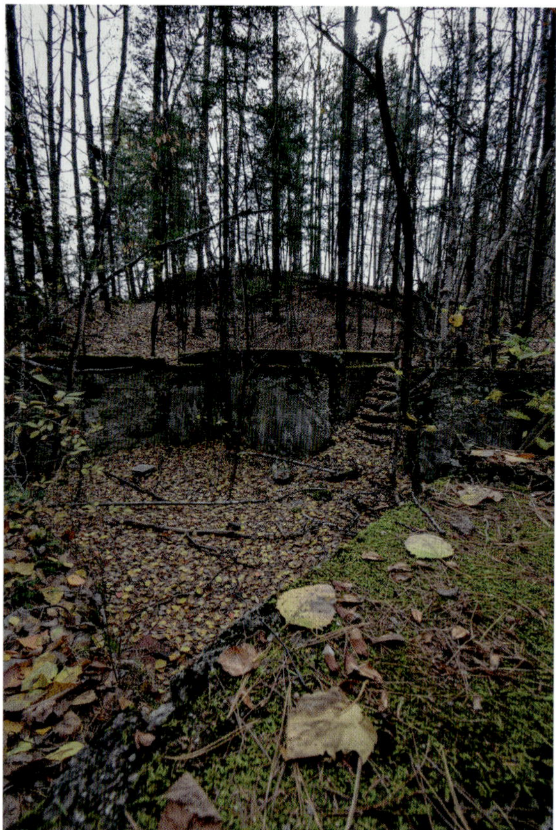

Foundations of the last hotel to be built on the land.

2

WHEN THE VACATION ENDS

Scattered across Vermont and throughout the mountains of New Hampshire, there are abandoned tourist cabins, motels, inns, discarded signage, theme parks, and even train depots that serve as reminders of a time when tourism and family vacations were more commonplace in these rural towns. Once the popularity started to decline, many lost business and eventually shuttered their doors.

Tourist cabins, found in the White Mountains, were built in the 1930s by Raymond and Phyllis Kimball. Prior to the Kimballs building the Mountaineer Cabins, the Mt. Adams House, built in 1864, stood on the property and burned down in 1913. The property was owned by the Crawshaw family until around 1920 when the Kimballs purchased it. The Mountaineer Cabins are mostly all standing to some degree. Some of the chimneys have fallen, scattering pieces of brick. Some of the porches, where guests once sat, have caved in. Each cabin was seemingly unique, offering a different experience for the guests. They sit with mountains, which used to draw many tourists, in the background.

Tourist cabins, often family owned, offered a unique alternative to staying in a normal motel or hotel room. And these little cabins, with affordable amenities, brought great memories to the people who stayed there. You will still find many places that still offer visitors the option of staying in tourist cabins, but sadly, there aren't as many still standing as there were in the past. It would also seem that the rise in private vacation rental properties has also played a role in the decline of motels and tourist cabins over the past decade or so.

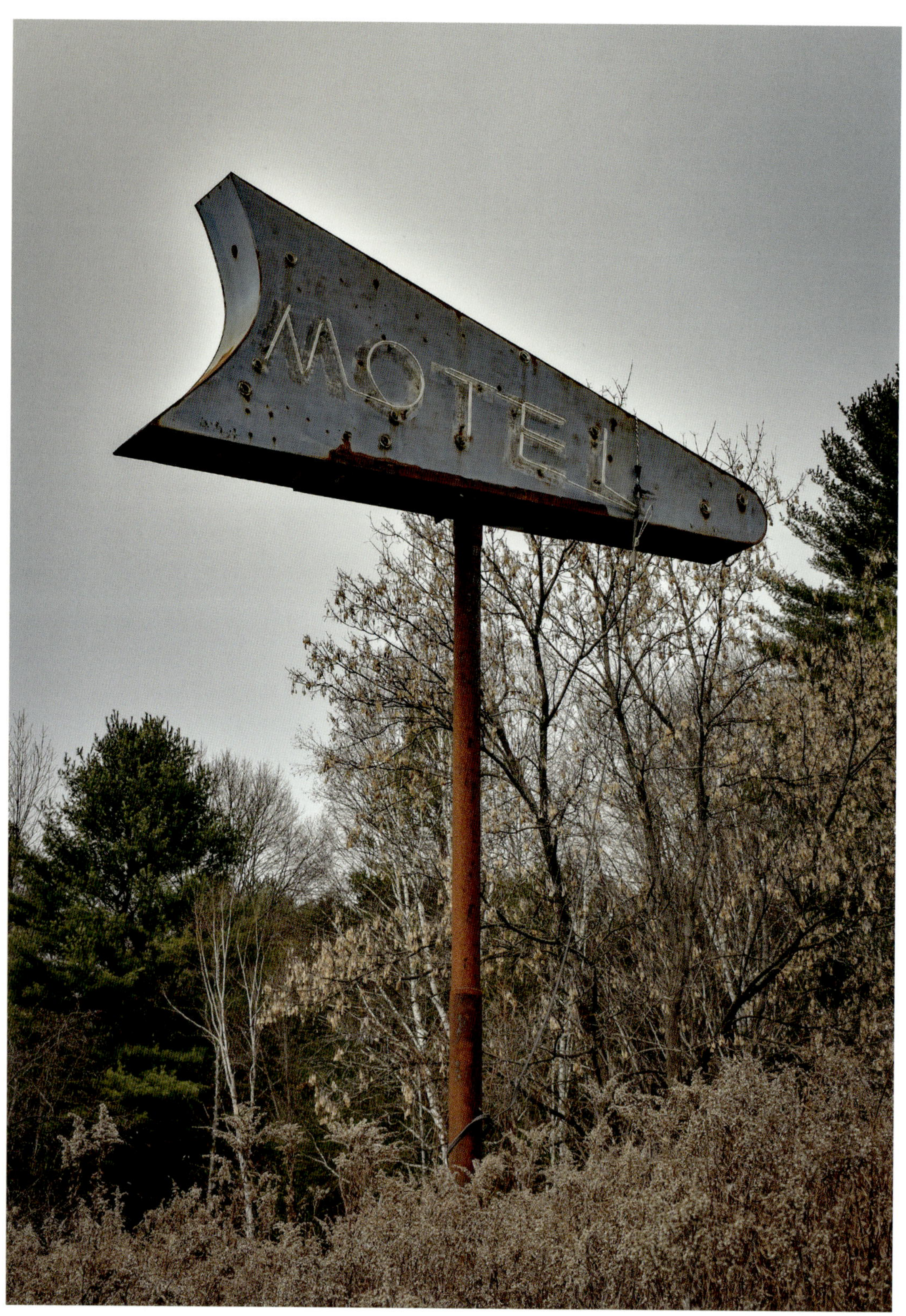

The motel sign is still standing, but the motel is long gone.

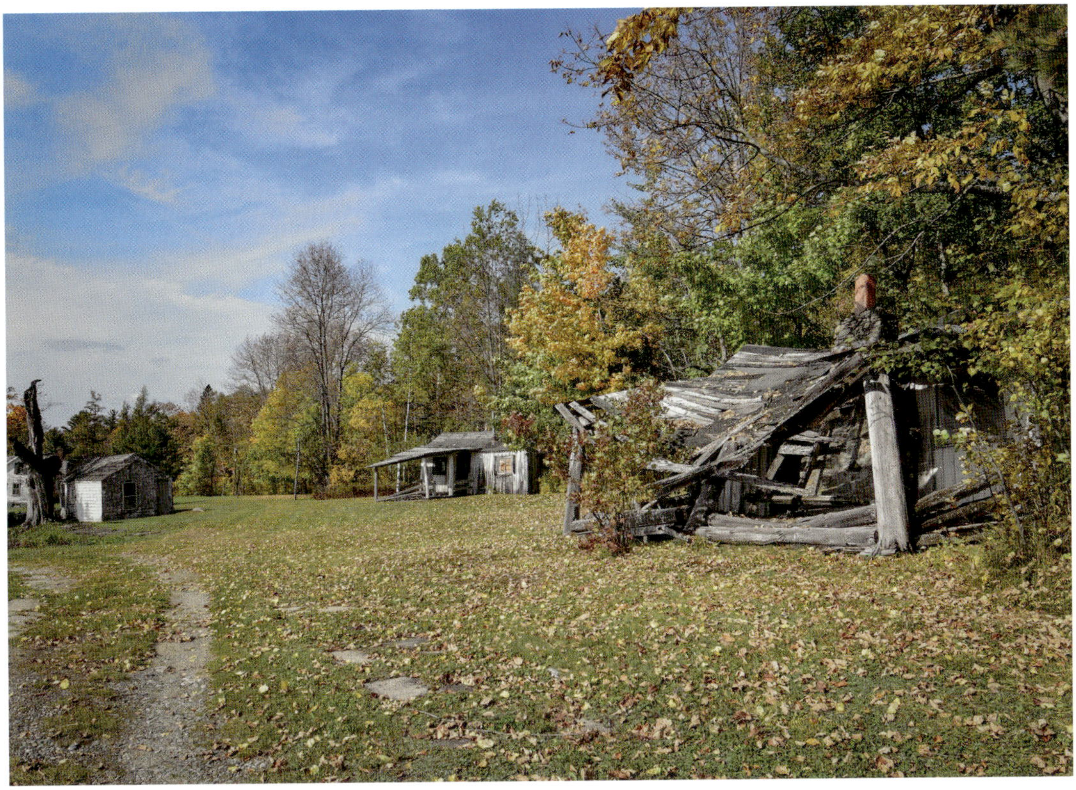

Mountaineer Cabins built in the 1930s.

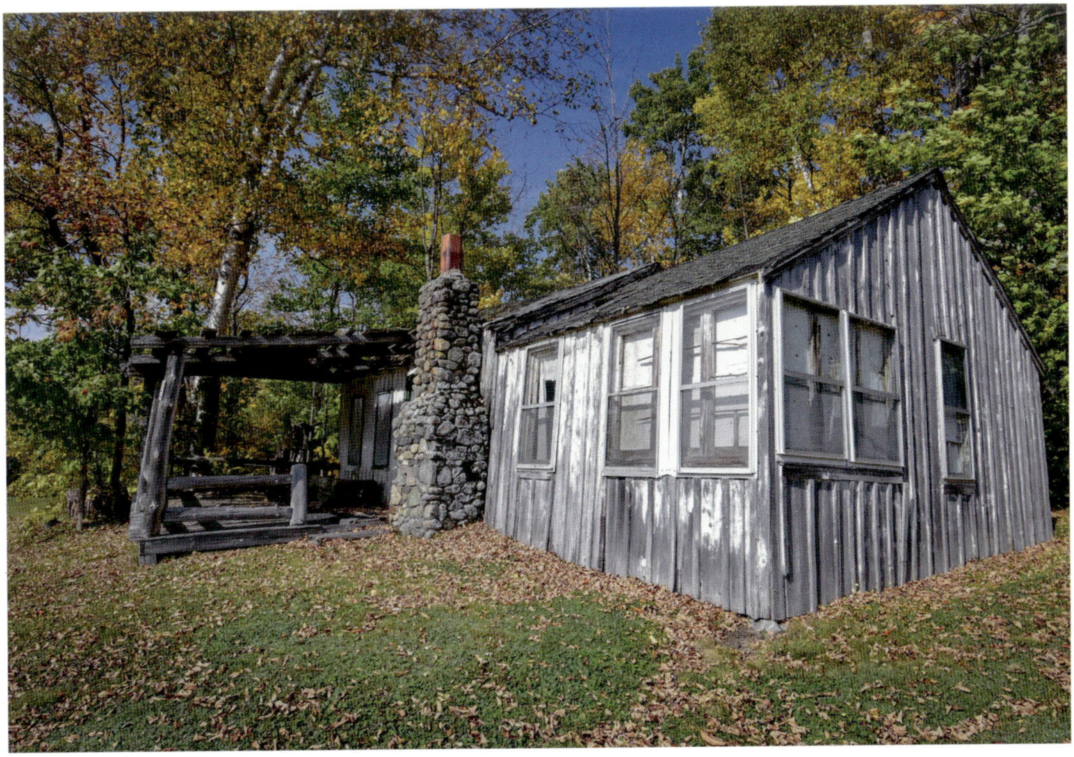

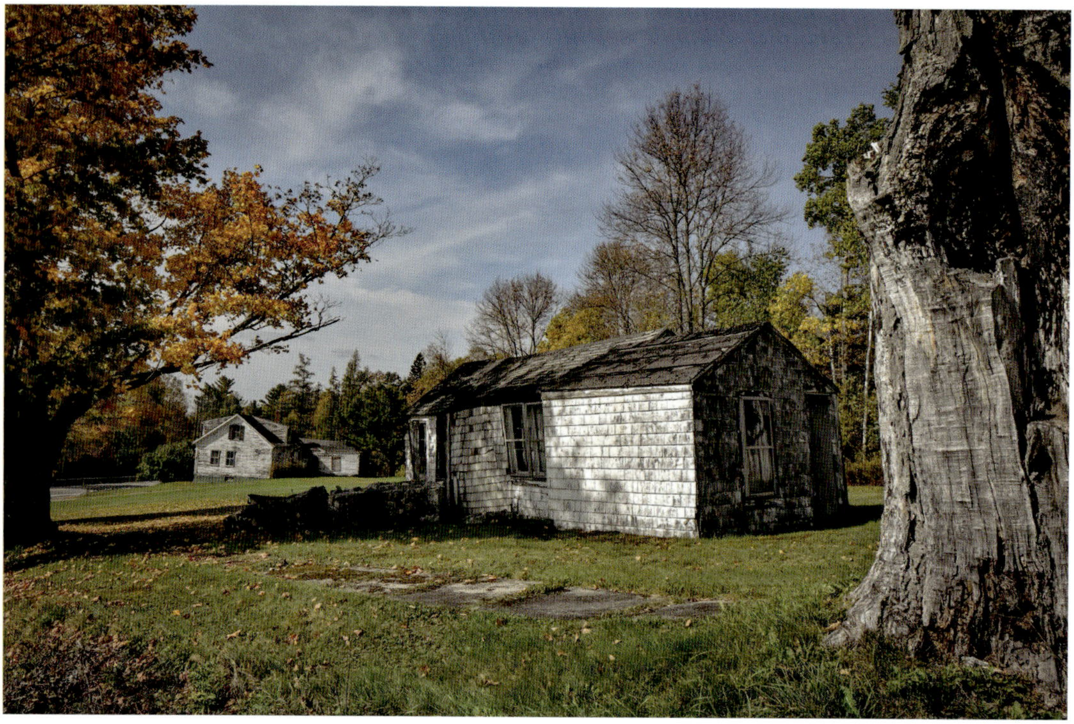

Mountaineer Cabins built in the 1930s.

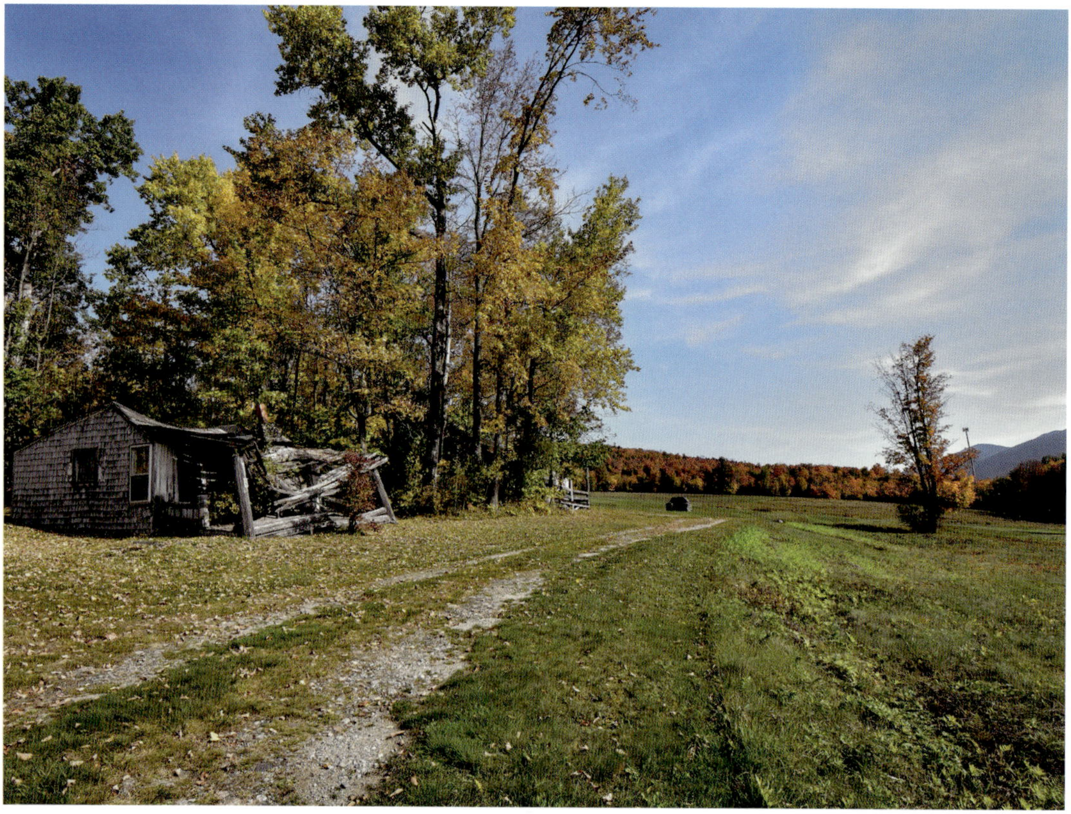

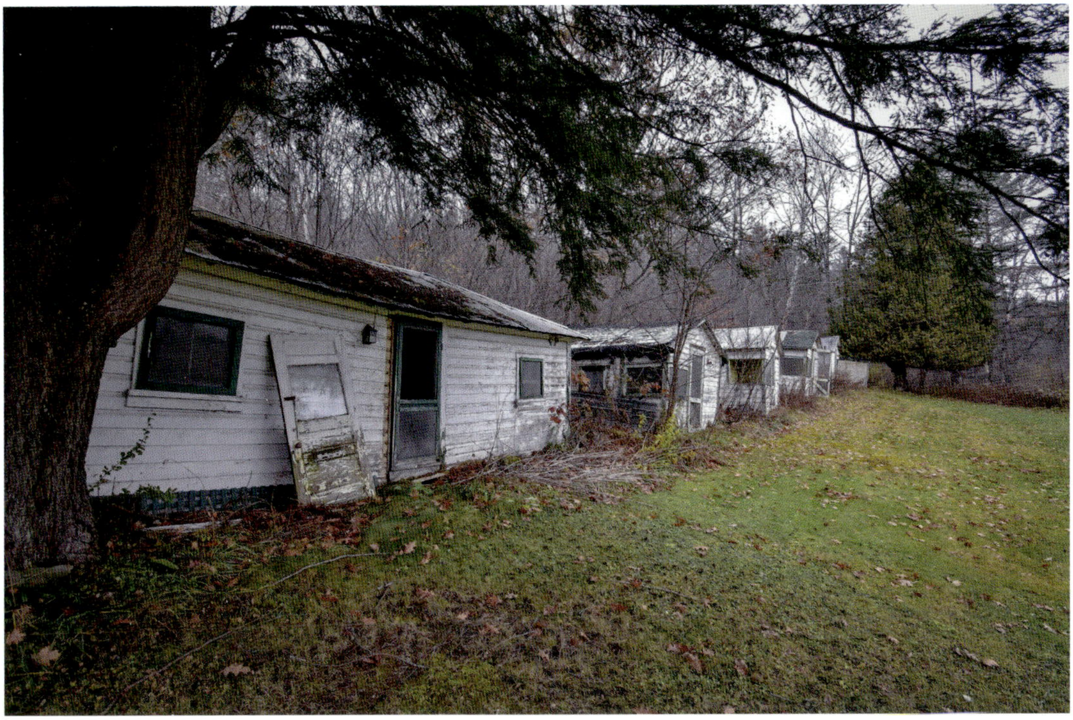

Above: Vermont tourist cabins.

Right: Inside one of the Vermont tourist cabins.

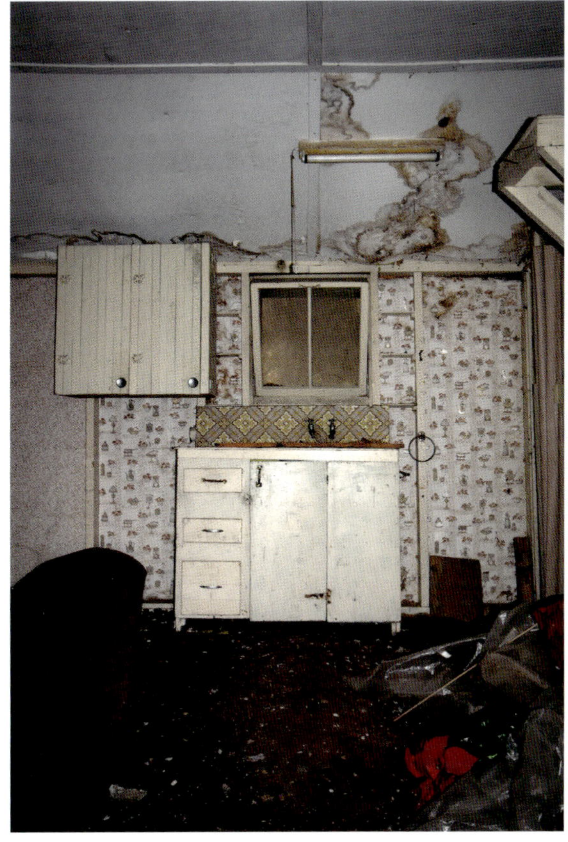

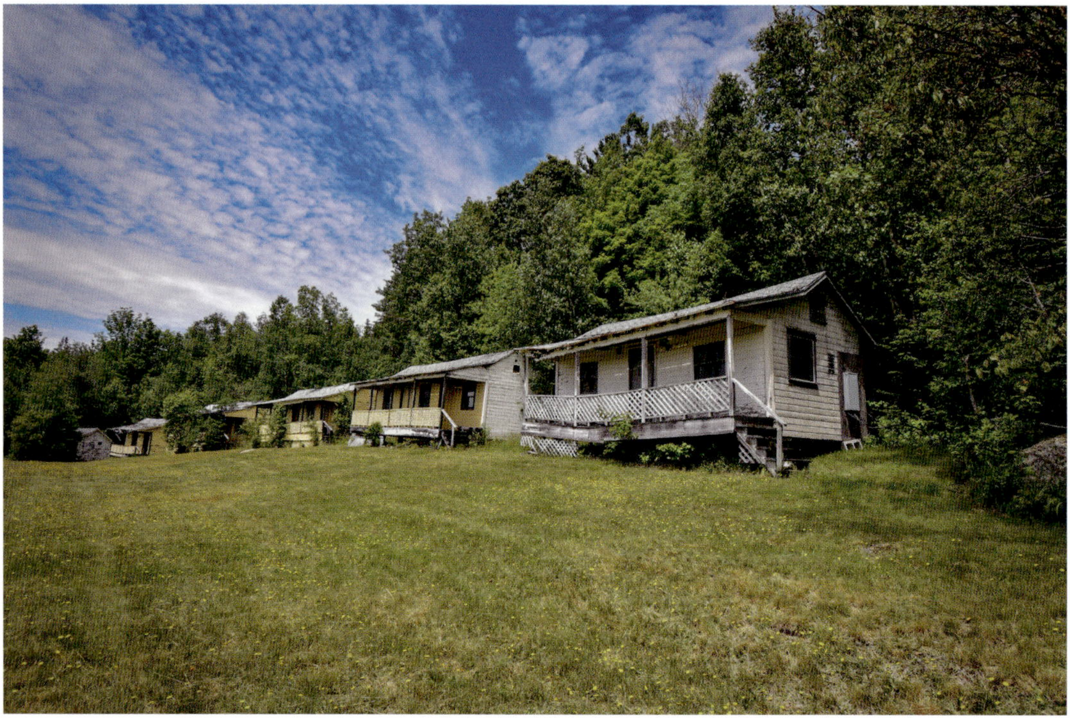

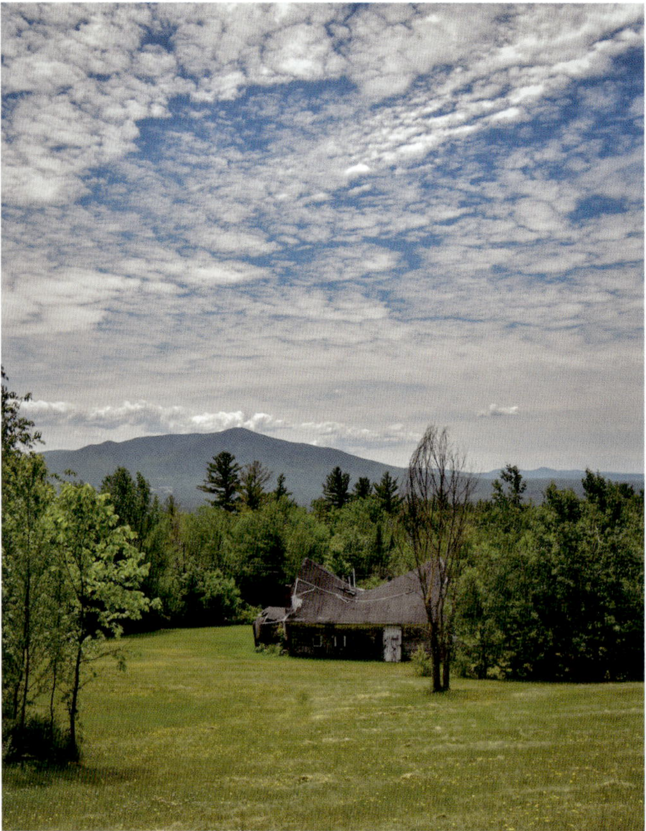

Chester Lodge and Cabins.

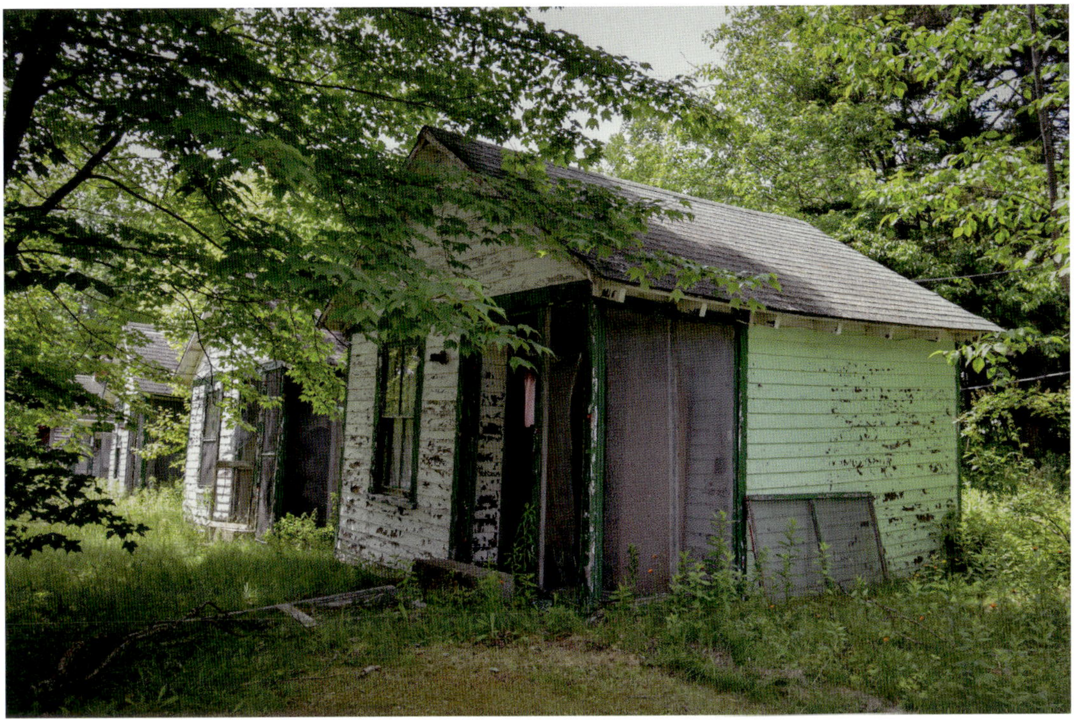

Above: More abandoned tourist cabins in the White Mountains.

Right: Chippy paint on the abandoned tourist cabins in the White Mountains.

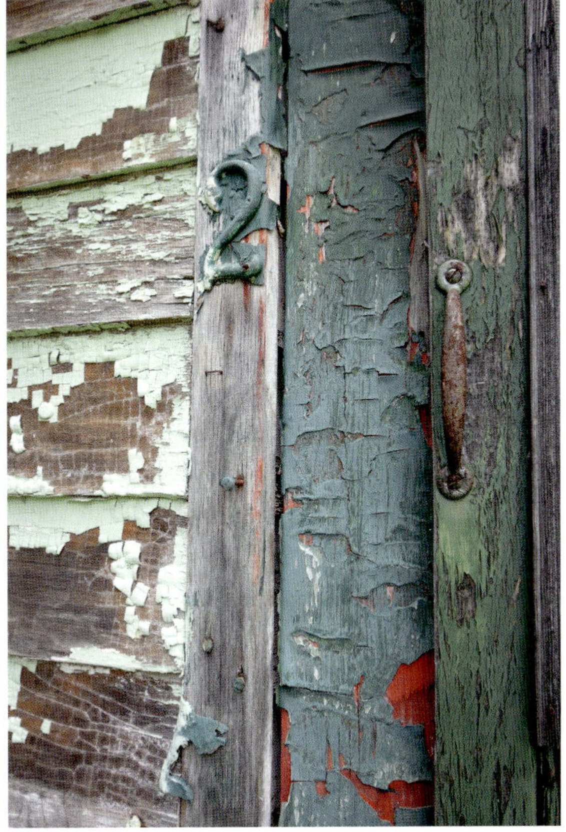

In a quiet, unincorporated community in New Hampshire, if you blink, you may miss the very faded sign for the inn that once welcomed guests to the grand building on the hill. I was fortunate to speak to a family member of the last owner of the inn. Giacomo "Jack" Iozzo was a veteran of the Korean War who had a great love for cooking, which he brought with him into his life as an innkeeper. His family, and many guests, including regulars, spent many vacations there, finding comfort and company in the gathering space Jack offered. Jack kept a garden outside and would make delicious meals out of the things he grew. Unfortunately, he eventually fell ill and had to leave his beloved inn behind. He walked out one day, and left things just as they were, including a full bar and kitchen as well as set tables. Sadly, Jack passed away not long after. Years later, Jack's grandniece went back to the inn to gather family photos and mementos. The ceiling had already started collapsing in various spots, but the photos of family and regular inn guests remained where Jack had left them. The large, red-carpeted staircase that undoubtedly many people who had been to the inn would remember, was blanketed in years of dust. She grabbed some family photos and other items, including a ladle—the perfect memento to honor a man who loved to cook. The years haven't been kind to Jack's forgotten inn, but the many memories that people made there certainly reflect well on a man who brought joy to others.

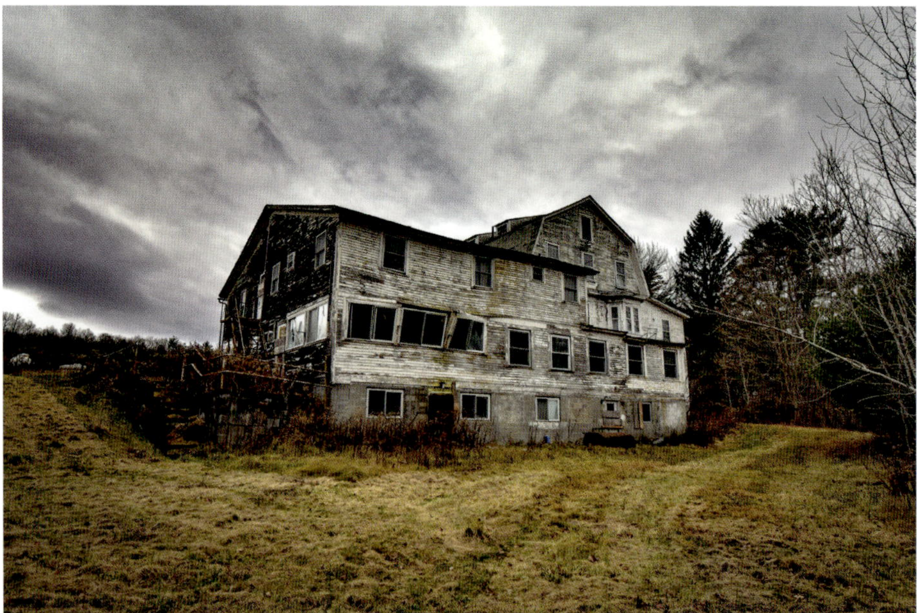

Towne House Inn – back.

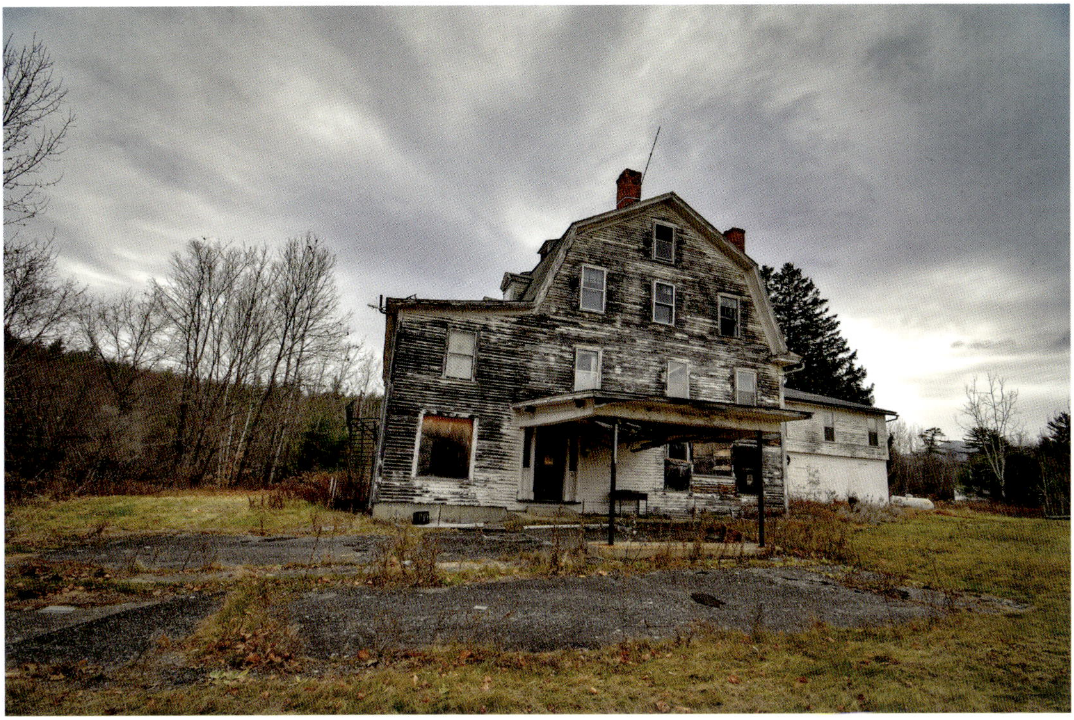

Above: Towne House Inn – front.

Right: A bench that used to be a spot for guests to rest at the Towne House Inn.

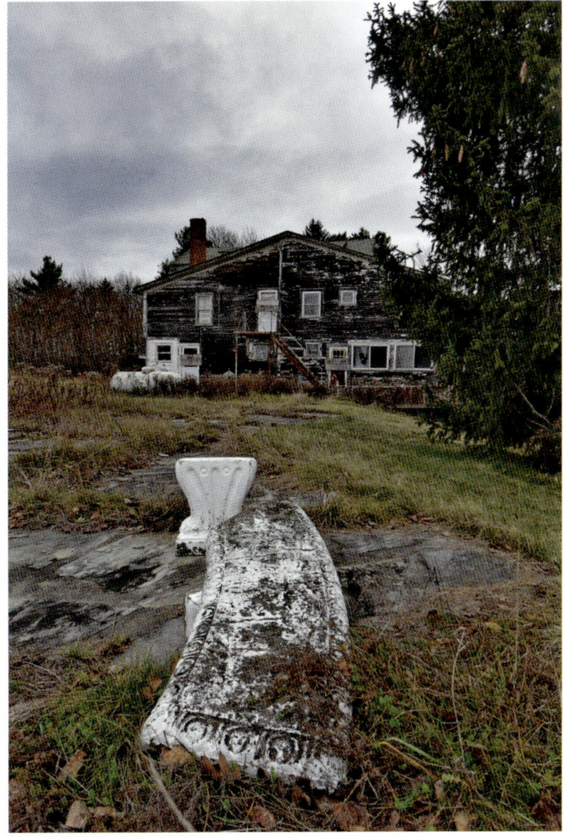

When you drive through the White Mountains, there doesn't seem to be a shortage of motels, inns, and campgrounds for visitors who come to spend their time surrounded by mountainous views and the woods. Some of these places, however, are no longer accepting visitors. They have long since closed their doors. The Charlmont Motor Inn Motel is one such place. Though its doors have been closed for quite some time now, the somehow well-kept vintage metal playground behind the motel looks as if kids could come back any minute to play on the slide, or swing on the swings.

Driving through Main Street in Bethlehem, NH, you will come across breathtaking Victorian homes—with giant, wrap-around porches, intricate woodwork, and turrets standing tall. But, in a stark juxtaposition, just down the street, you will also see stretches of abandonment that brings you back to a time when the area saw more tourism and families enjoying the shops, beautiful lakes, and all that the White Mountains have to offer.

One of these abandoned beauties was the old Maplewood Depot. The depot, which was one of three in the area, brought people, many of them well-known and affluent (presidents, authors, artists, etc.), into town. It also brought others who were set on building summer homes for their families. During the peak of tourist season, as many as eight to ten trains came into Bethlehem per day.

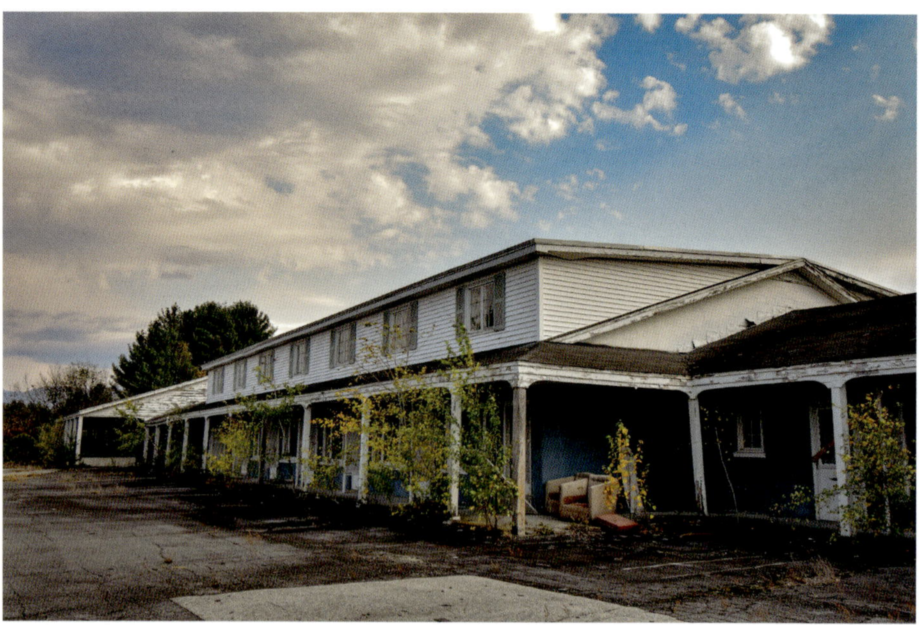

Charlmont Motor Inn Motel.

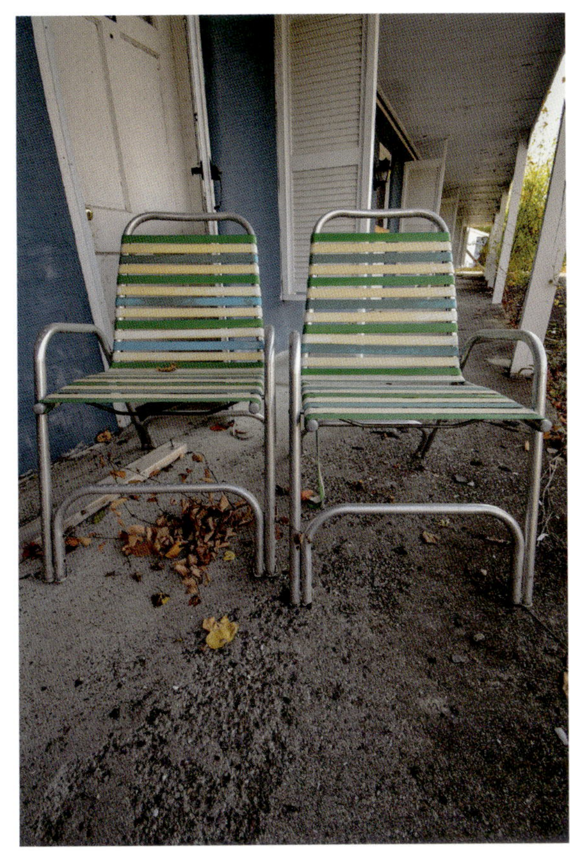

Right: Abandoned chairs Charlmont Motor Inn Motel.

Below: Ice and soda room.

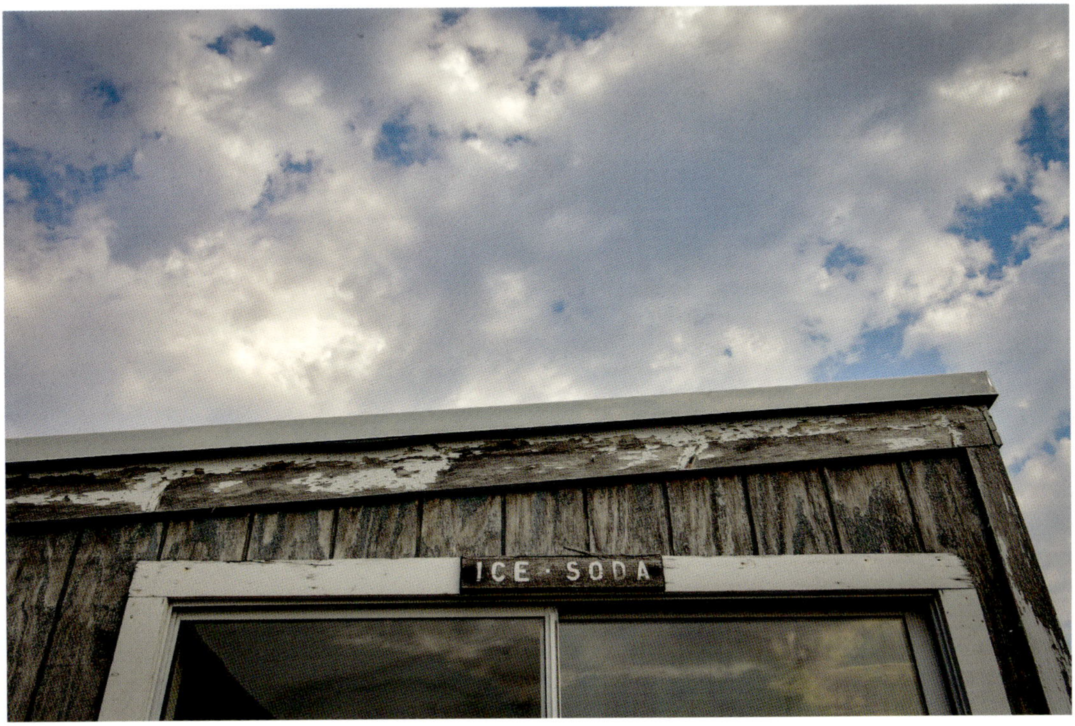

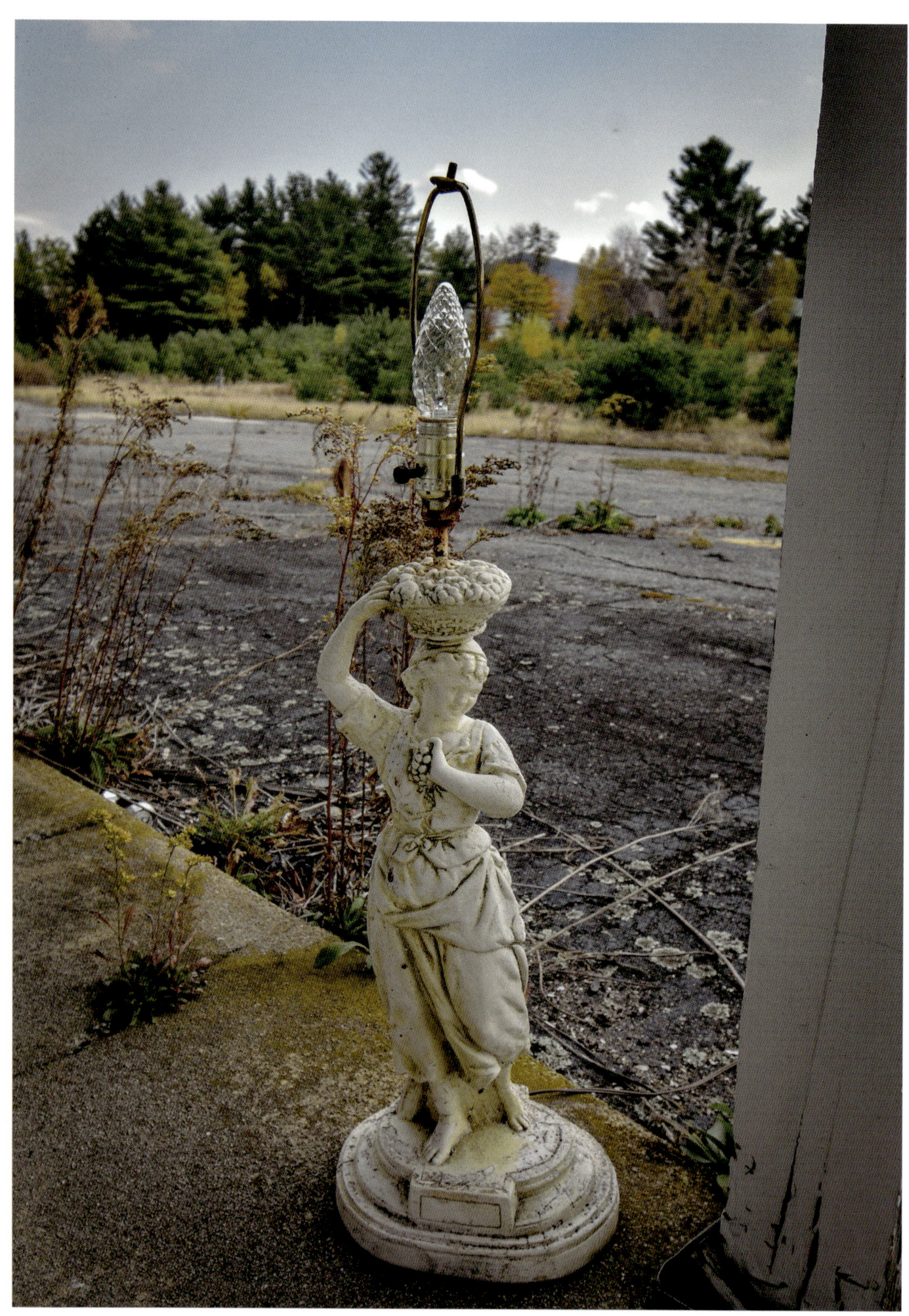

A discarded lamp stands outside of one of the empty rooms.

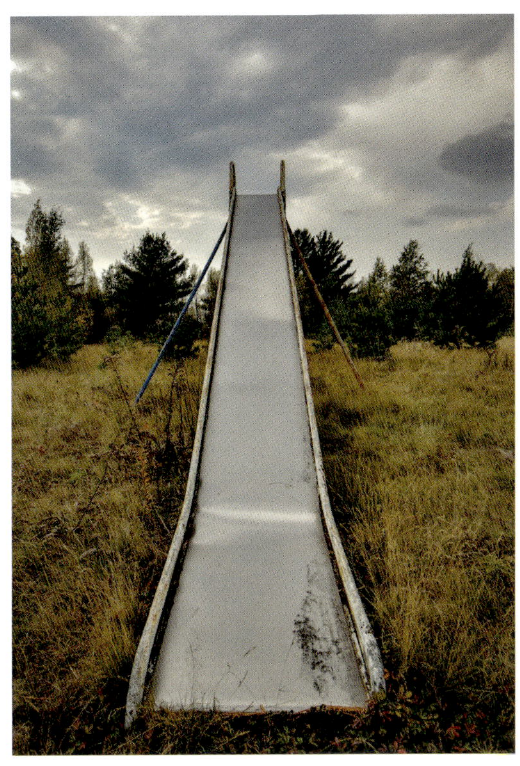

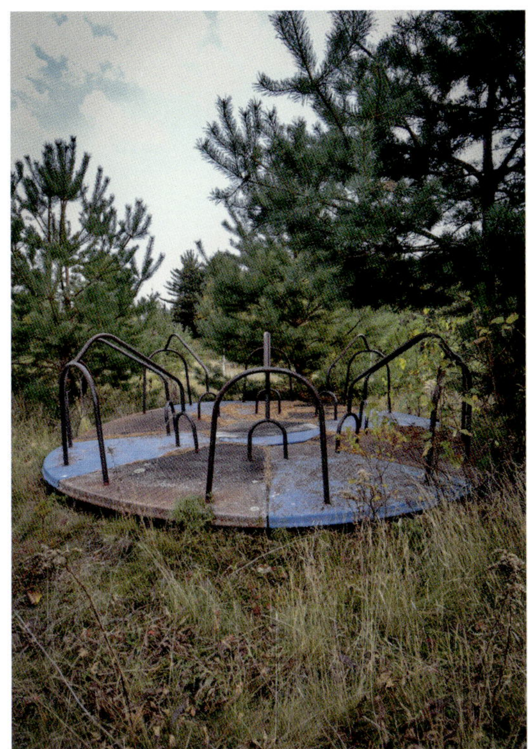

Above left: Vintage metal slide.

Above right: Vintage, rusting roundabout. How many kids took a spin on this?

Right: Vintage painted horse glider swing set.

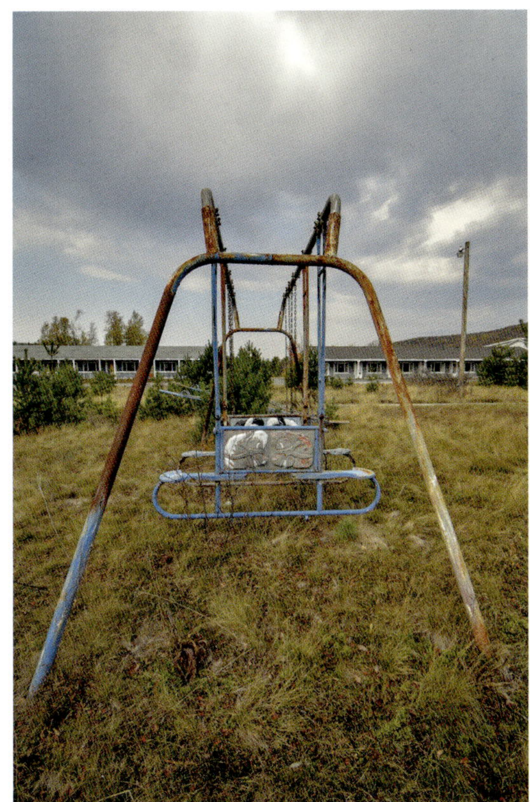

Sadly, once tourism started to dwindle, and automobiles started gaining popularity, the train depot was eventually abandoned in the early 1920s. And abandoned is how it has existed for almost 100 years. When I finally saw it, I was in awe of how, despite the sagging of the upper floor and the hard, almost haunting lean of the structure itself, and despite it having no intact windows or doors, it was still standing. Life hasn't been kind to it during these harsh northern seasons. But the fact that it withstood almost 100 winters since its abandonment is a true testament to the craftsmanship of the past. The depot saw its final days when it was finally razed in 2021, with plans of moving what could be salvaged and rebuilding closer to the center of town.

When tourism starts to drop in certain areas, motels, hotels, and tourist cottages aren't the only things that start to suffer. Once busy restaurants, theme parks, and stores also feel the impact of the loss of business.

One place that has seen the effects of the dwindling tourist industry in the area is the once loved Six Gun City in the White Mountains. Six Gun City was a frontier, western theme park that started welcoming families in 1954. When the park first opened, there were family-friendly events such as stagecoach and pony rides and skits. Later, in the 80s and 90s, water rides were added to the park, to keep up with the changing interests of tourists. Over time, go-carts, bumper boats, and a

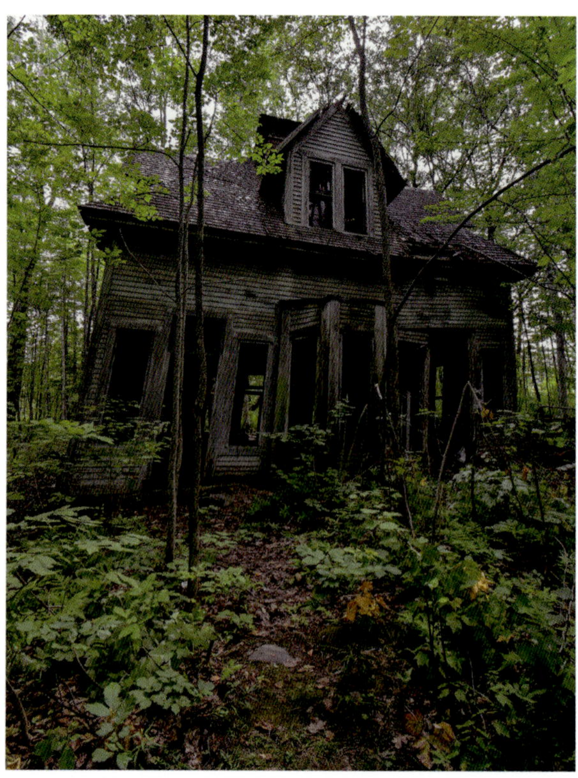

Maplewood Depot from the outside.

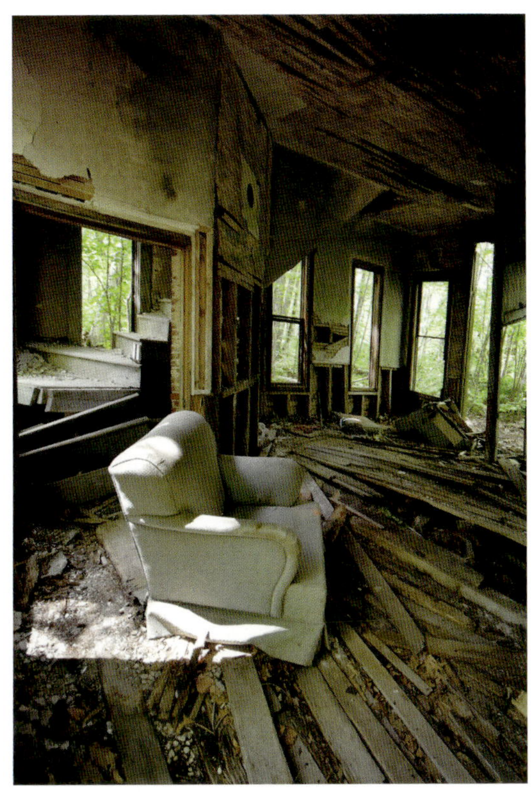

Maplewood Depot inside.

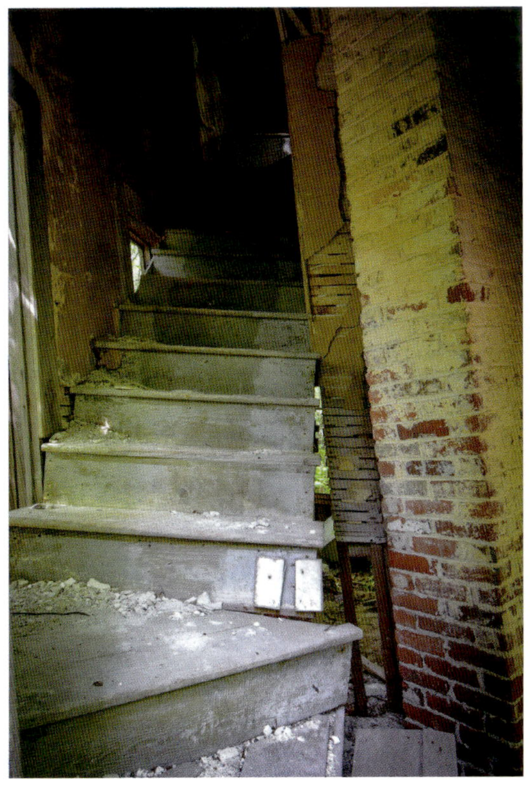

Maplewood Depot stairs going up to the now collapsed top floor.

train roller coaster were also added. In 2014, the name of the park changed to Fort Jefferson Fun Park and Campground, when the focus shifted to it becoming more of a fun park than a theme park, but much of what was loved at Six Gun City remained. Though it permanently closed not long after it was renamed, everything remains standing, keeping the memories made there intact.

When the Barefoot Boy of Baker Brook Restaurant was built in the late 1940s, it drew tourists who wanted to visit the beautiful White Mountains. Both the restaurant and the small Baker Brook cabins were always filled with vacationing families. Purchased by new owners in the 80s, some updates were made and then it was left to fall apart. There are no reminders of the vibrancy of the Barefoot Boy remaining—just a dreary, crumbling building and postcards from a much happier time. The cabins, now rebuilt, have received new life, and are once again welcoming new visitors.

After doing a little research, I discovered an abandoned structure I initially thought was a house was actually once a maple farm, which had a gift shop and maple museum and, from what I heard, delicious pancakes as well. Christie's Maple Farm is situated in what was seemingly once a great location for tourists. Across the road from the maple farm is a campground and motel. It seems that the motel, however, has also seen better days. There's a defunct mini golf course that looks as if it hasn't seen any golfers in years. Not far down the road are a couple of theme parks, one of which was mentioned earlier in the chapter. I'm not sure why this place closed, but seeing it, along with the many other now abandoned places where people have spent their family vacations, reminds me of the fact that times change, and it's not always feasible to keep up with it all. The world around us keeps going, and it keeps changing, and sometimes we end up with these now lonely places that people drive by and feel a sense of sadness and nostalgia.

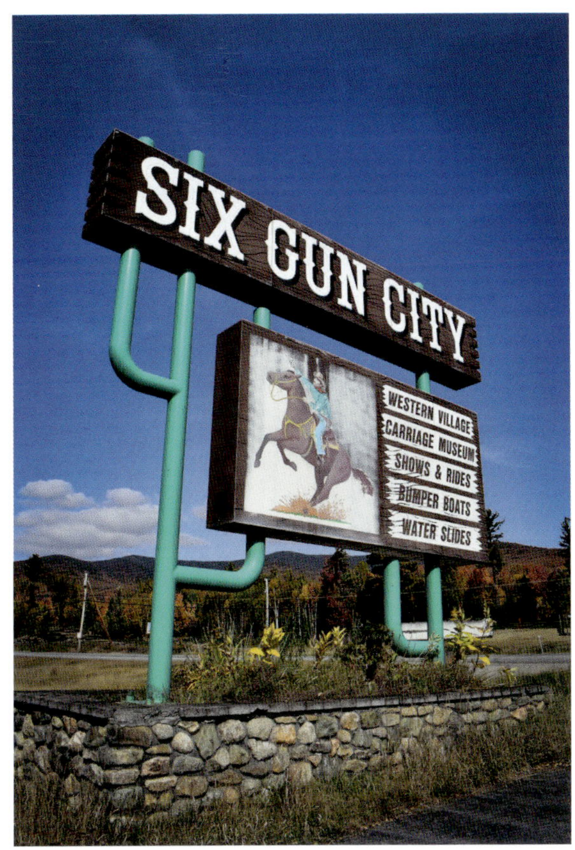

Right: Six Gun City sign.

Below: Some of the abandoned buildings at Six Gun City.

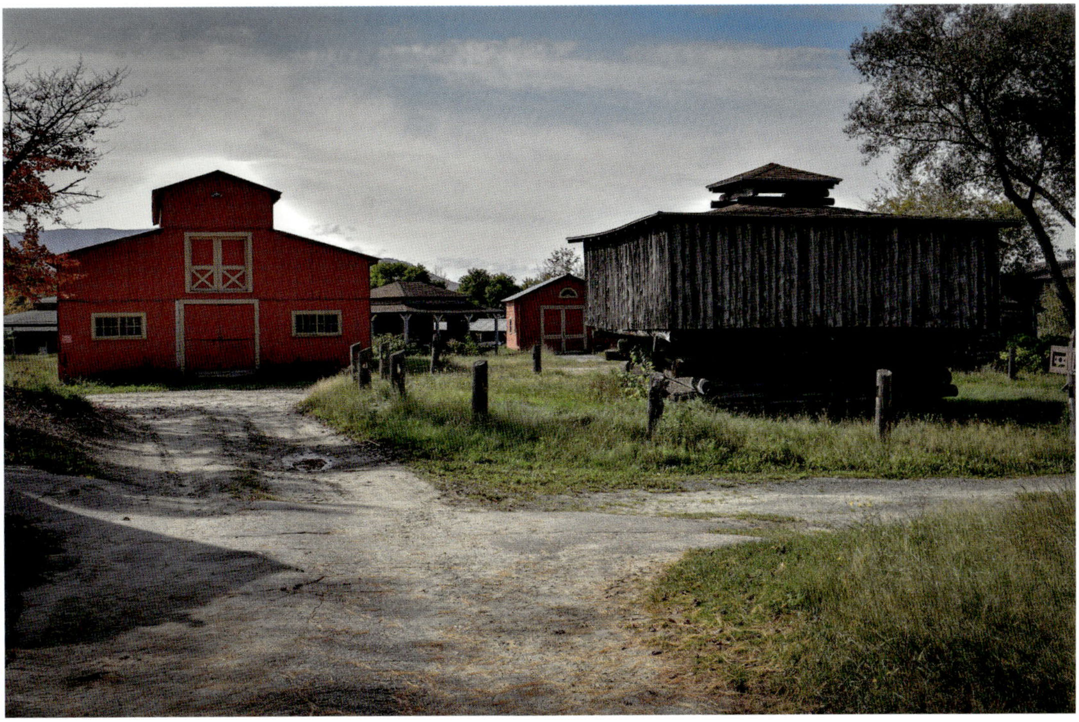

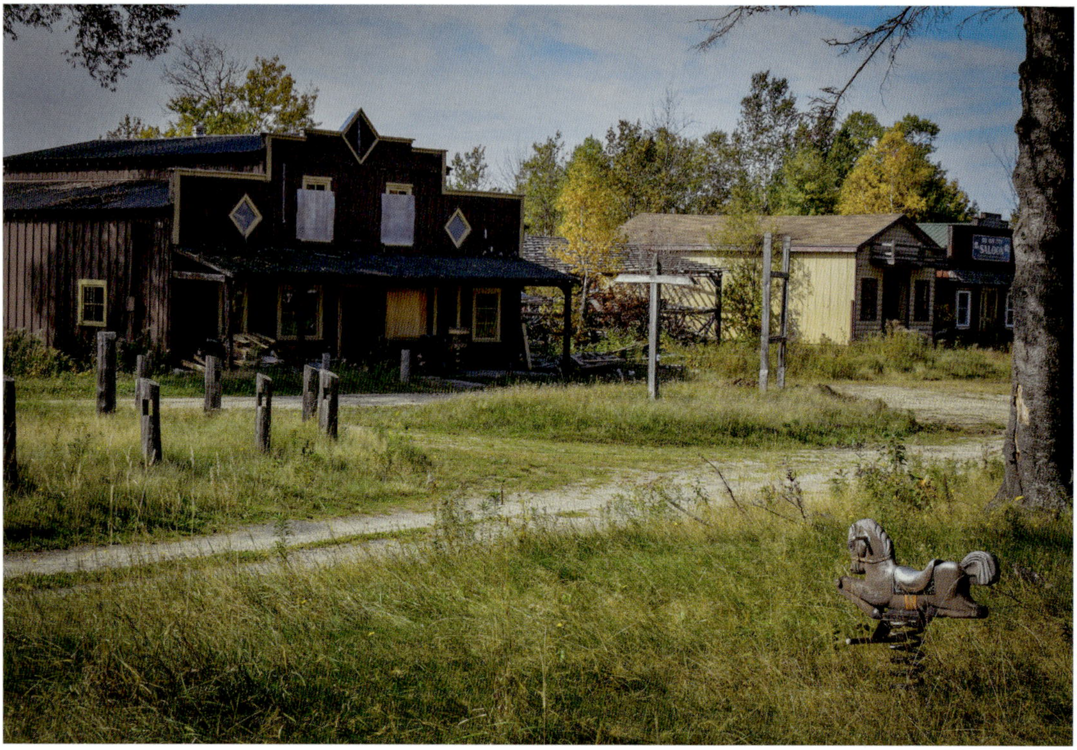

A lone spring rider horse watches over the abandoned buildings at Six Gun City.

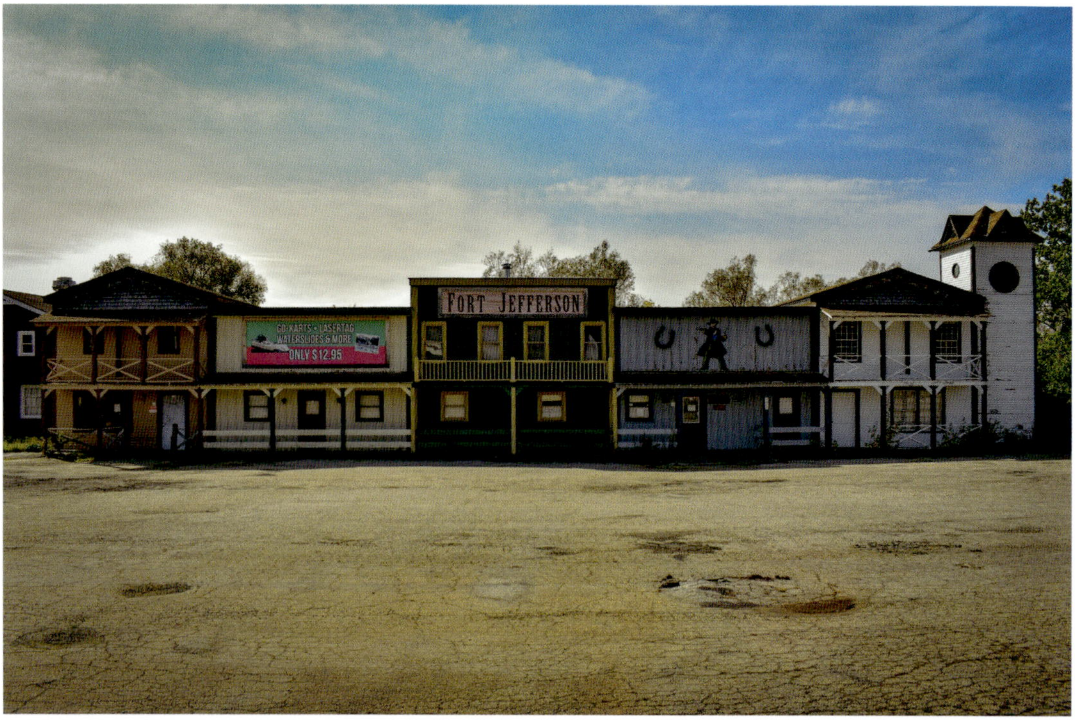

Six Gun City buildings that used to welcome tourists.

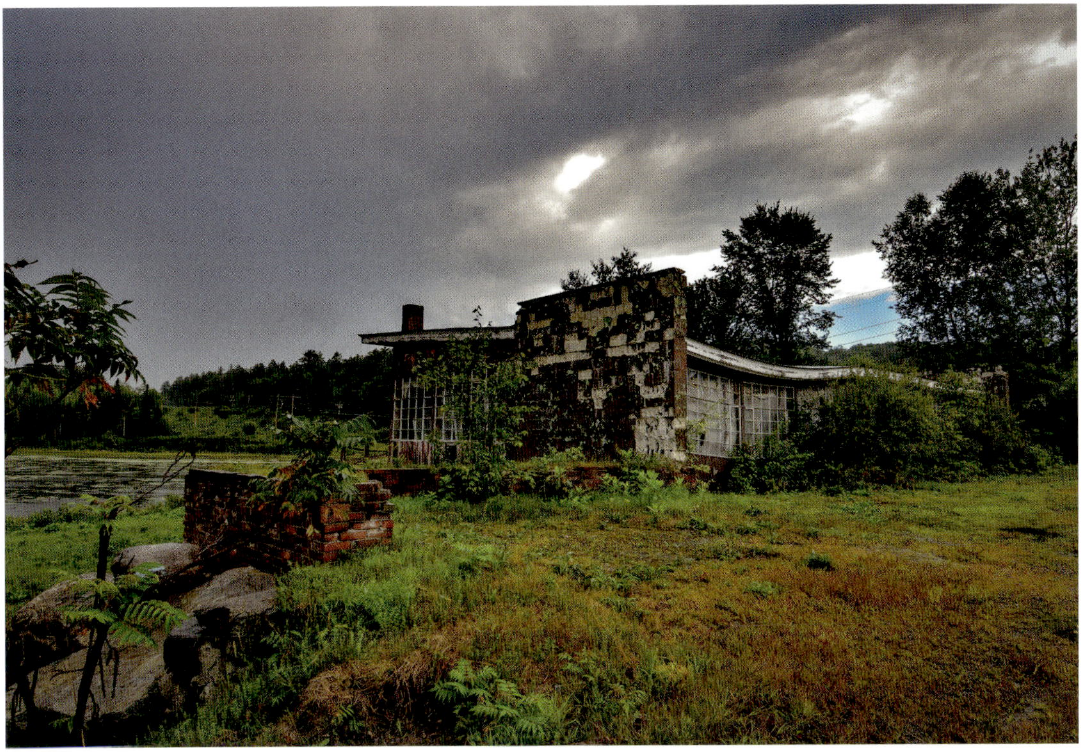

Above: What's left of the Barefoot Boy of Baker Brook restaurant.

Right: Christie's Maple, which at first glance looks like a house, was once a bustling Maple Farm.

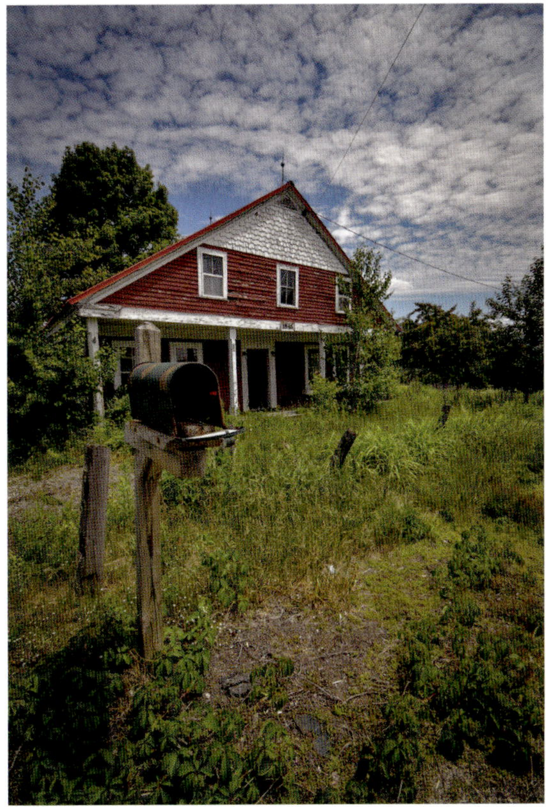

3

UNTIL THE WHEELS FALL OFF

There's something about rust. Seeing abandoned and discarded vehicles on farms, the side of the road, or even in the woods, is commonplace in rural areas. I often wonder how many of these rusted beauties started off as well-intentioned projects, and somewhere in the process, life just kind of got in the way. In some instances, farmland has become less tended, and some of it has gone back to nature, taking with it anything that may not have been moved in a while. Some have been parked and left with the hopes that they will one day be used again, but "one day" never seems to come. Various modes of transportation hold great significance for people, for countless reasons. There's freedom in the memories we make with the vehicles we love, and it's not always easy to part with them, so you hold on, and sometimes those memories start to rust. I think of my own memories I've made driving over the years, and how I am fortunate to be able to drive in order to do what I enjoy doing—which is shining a light, even briefly, on the discarded and forgotten in the places that surround me.

There are so many songs that remind me of my childhood—so many songs that remind me of drives in the car with my mom, singing along with the radio. I can't hear "Fast Car" by Tracy Chapman without hearing my mom's quiet, beautiful voice. You know those songs that put your heart and mind at ease? The ones that remind you of home for one reason or another? This will forever be one of mine. When I got my license and started driving, almost every playlist I ever made included this song, and when I hear it, the memories of those drives come flooding back. Like so many growing up, years of my life were also spent driving around aimlessly with my friends. During those drives, I had some of the most honest conversations I've ever had with anyone—as if the car somehow became a moving confessional. There was something freeing about being there, in those moments. Years later, I find myself thinking about some of those moments when I'm driving.

It's sometimes hard seeing tangible reminders of our past start to fall apart. All the old cars, bicycles, boats, tractors, ATVs, and trucks that you may see in someone's yard are just a collection of their memories from some point in their life, a souvenir of who they were then, just in the form of a rusty memorial.

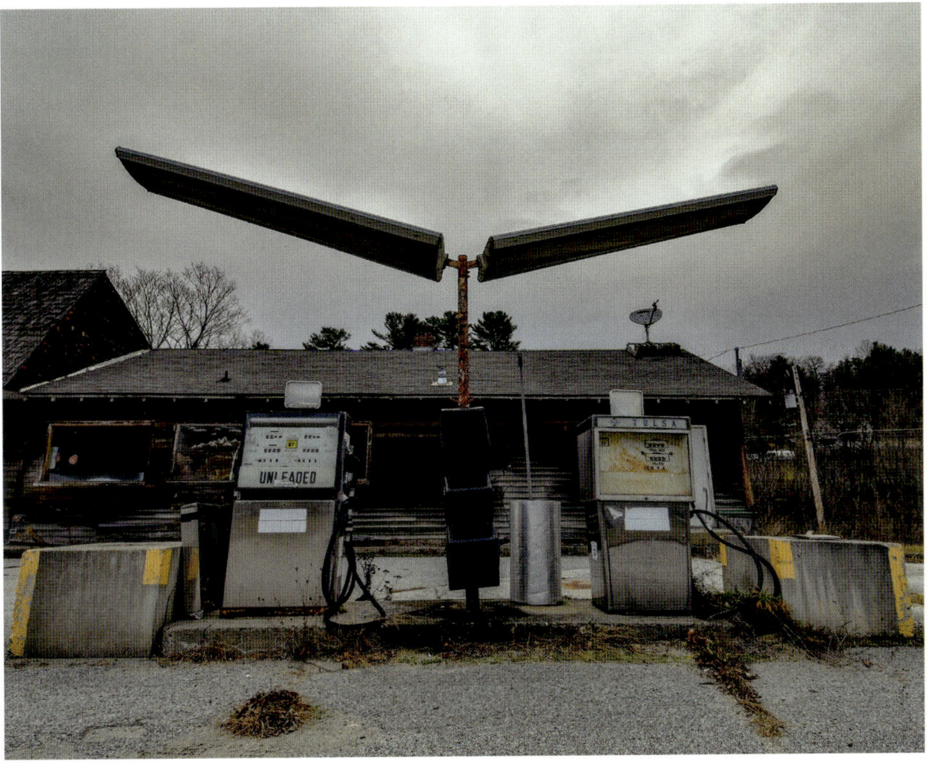

Abandoned gas station.

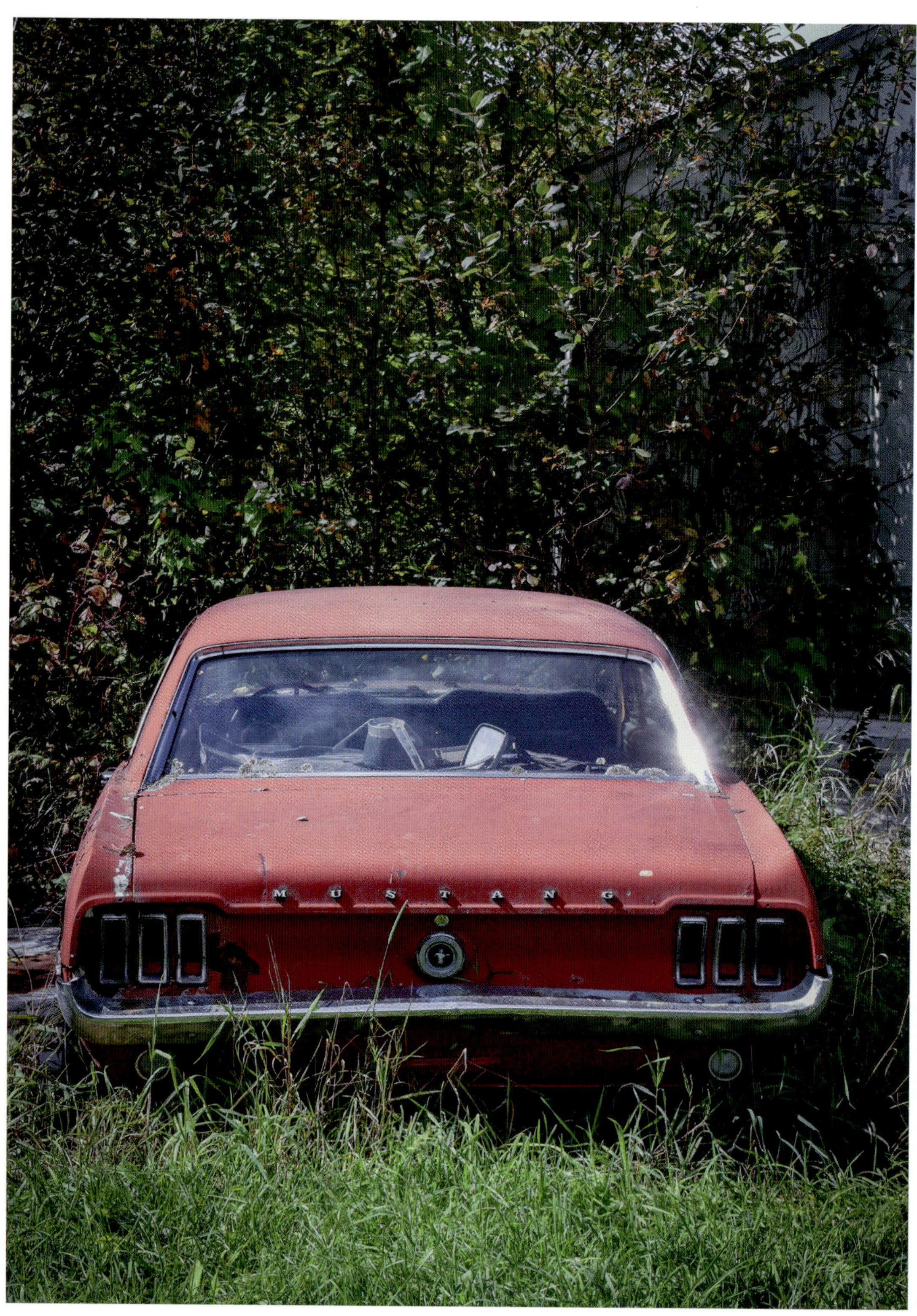

This Mustang hasn't seen the road in a while.

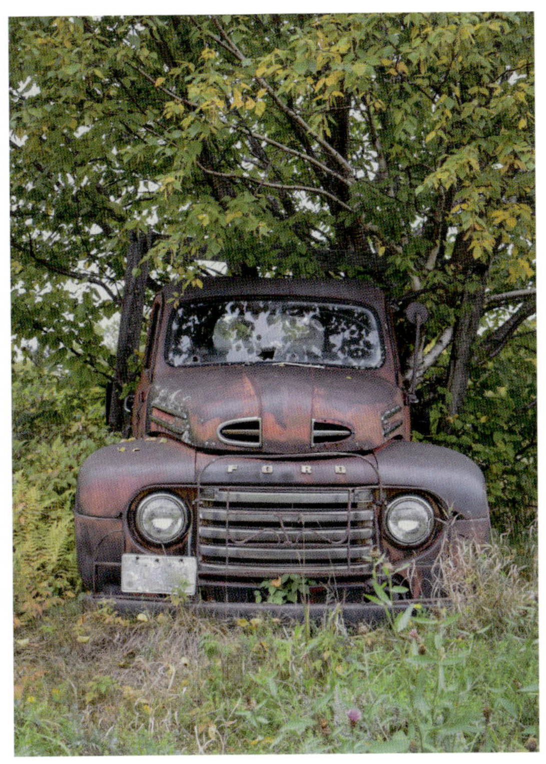

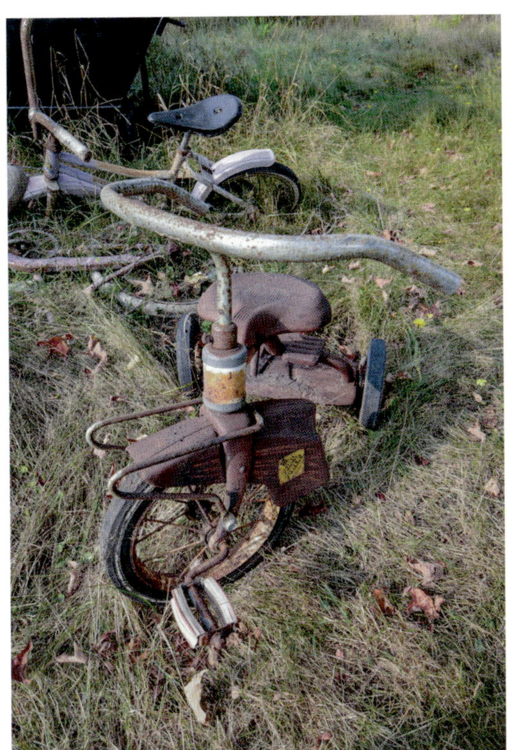

Above left: Backed into the trees, this farm truck sits with a broken window and a rusting hood.

Above right: A rusty tricycle sits among a pile of bikes with a 1981 Burger King Pedal Power reflector sticker.

Right: A discarded Edsel sits on the side of the road.

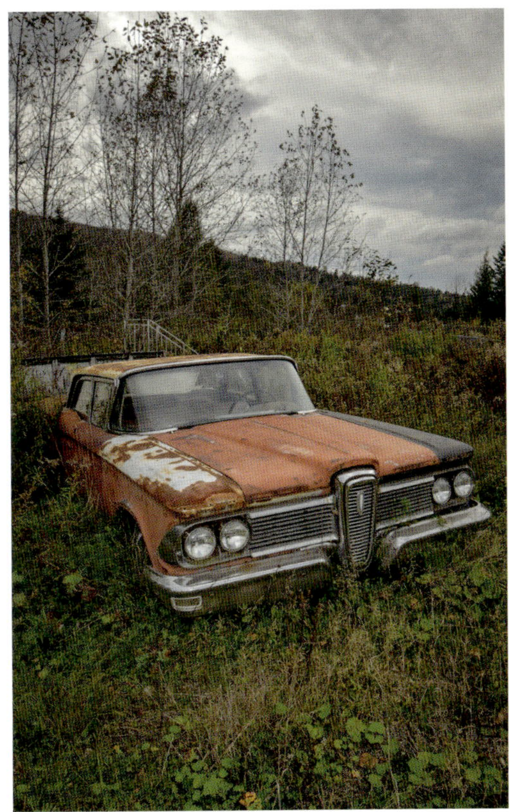

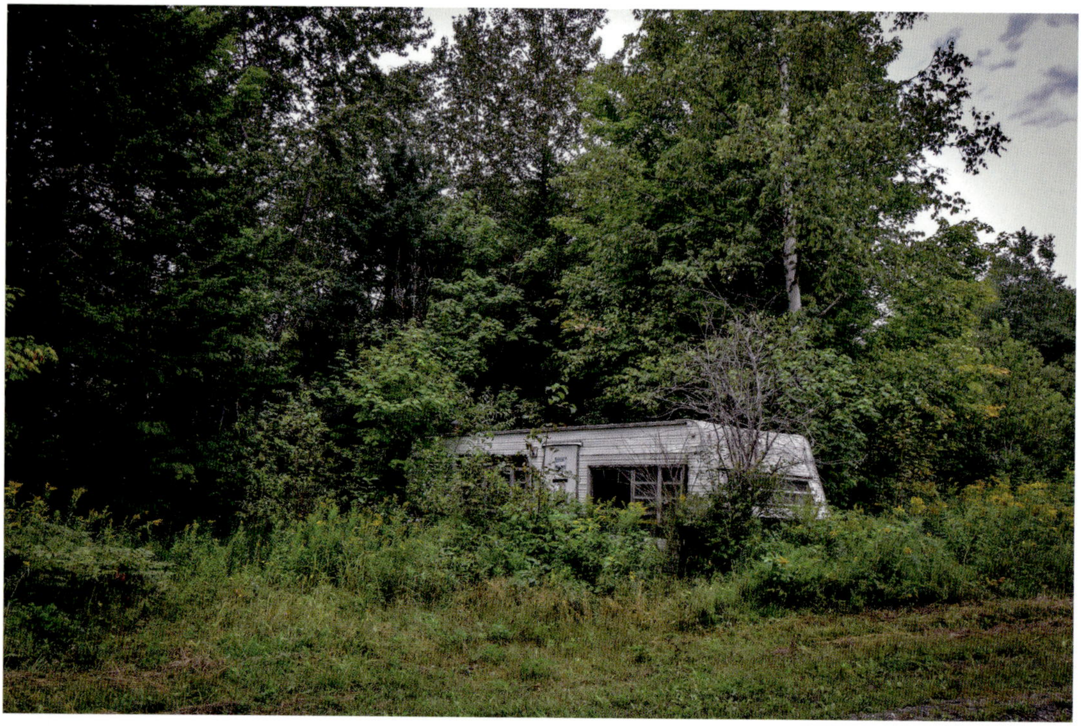

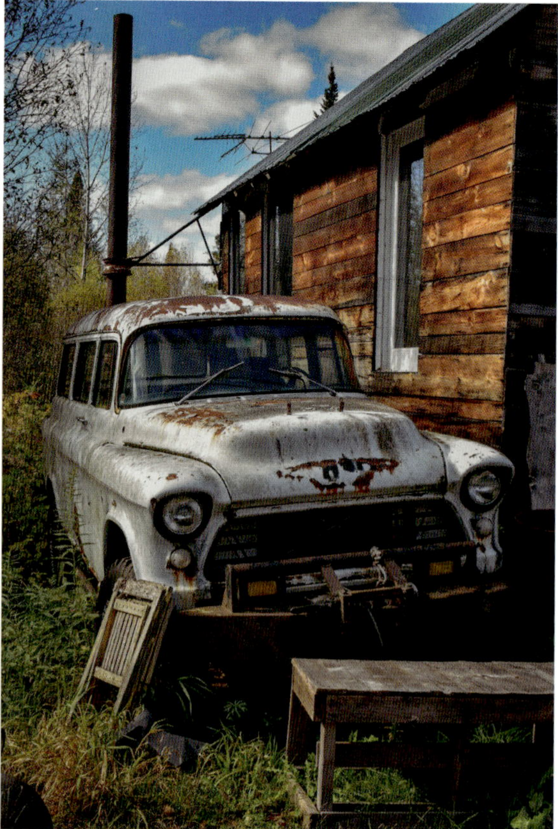

Above: Abandoned campers are a common sight to see in the woods.

Left: A rusting 1950s Chevy Suburban.

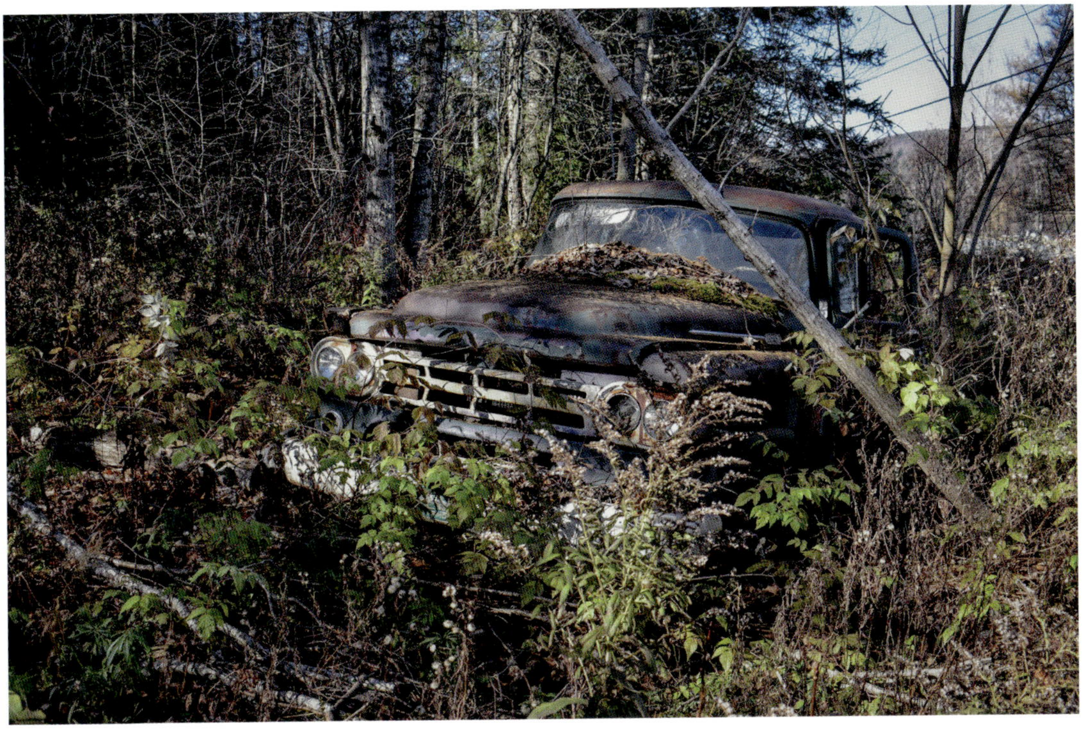

Above: Abandoned in the woods.

Right: Hiding among the flowers.

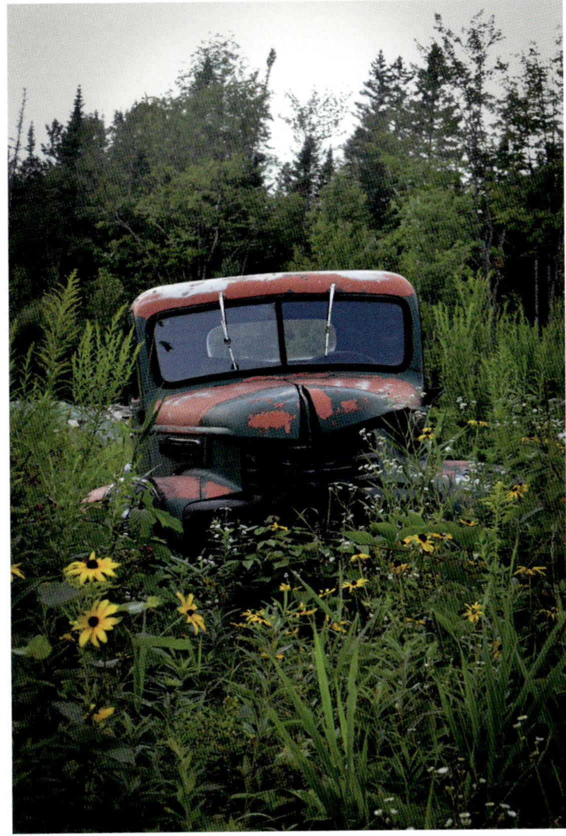

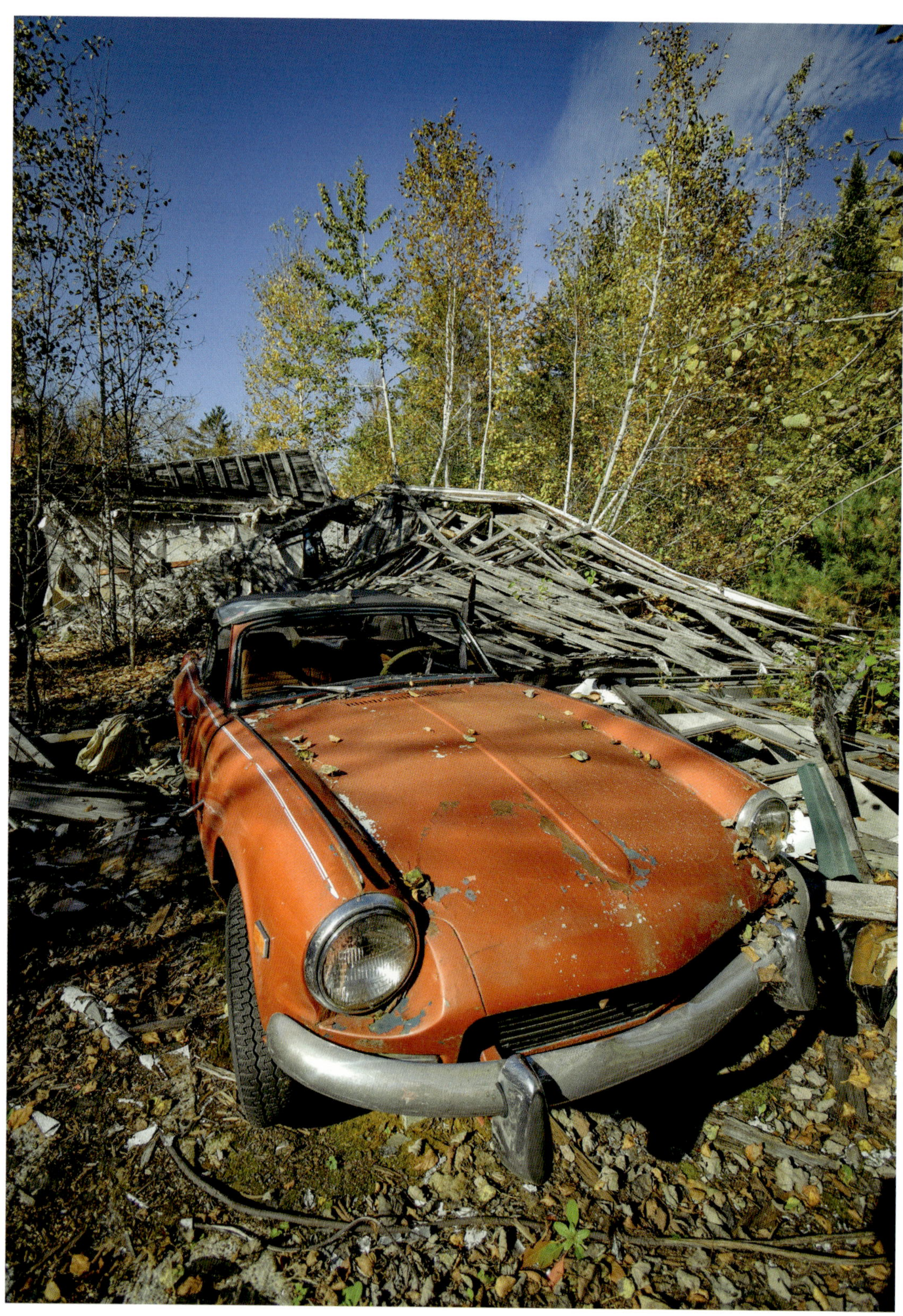

The garage has seemingly just fallen down around the car.

4

STORIES OF HOME

What many of these small, mountainous towns lack in population size, they often make up for in character and beautiful notches filled with long and interesting histories. Some things can be said about living in small towns, away from the noises of big cities and crowds of people. What I've learned from living in a small town is that there's a great deal of peace to be found in these places. It's easy to see how houses that are off the beaten path, on dirt roads with lush tree coverage or deep snow drifts, can spend years remaining hidden in the shadows. These old homes, now mostly taken over by moss and generations of overgrowth and creeping vines, are all in various stages of decay and disrepair, the once beautiful and strong architecture giving way to the makings of typical scary movie houses.

Built around 1920, this small, one-room schoolhouse had been sitting and falling apart in the northernmost town in New Hampshire for many years. Once it was no longer used as a schoolhouse, someone converted it to a private residence. Sadly, it had to be torn down and the all-too-familiar signs of land clearing have begun.

The land itself holds historical significance as well, being the spot where the Indian Stream Republic's Constitution was adopted. The Republic was founded after about sixty years of contention between the United States and Canada, due to a dispute over uncertain boundaries. The roughly 300 residents of the Republic took it upon themselves to declare that they were independent of both New Hampshire/U.S. and Canada. In doing so, they established their own constitution, laws, legislature, courts, and militia.

After quite a few incidents, including the arrest of a Republic leader in Canada and the subsequent "war," the New Hampshire state militia was ordered to occupy the Indian Stream Republic. In 1836, the citizens of the Republic accepted New Hampshire as their authority, becoming a part of Pittsburg. And in 1842, it was recognized by treaty as a territory of the United States.

The things that people leave behind when they go sometimes offer clues as to who they were, and the lives they lived. Random piles and drawers full of paper ghost photographs, curled at the corners, encased in dust, like spirits forever trapped in time. I always wonder how items like this, that should seemingly hold some significance to someone, can be so easily forgotten in these places. Not every abandoned house offers a decaying treasure trove of trinkets and proof of a live once lived, but when they do, it's hard not to pause and wonder if the well-used chair you're looking at was once someone's favorite. Or if the kitchen table, now covered in fallen insulation, was once where a family shared stories about their days. Or if the piles of books scattered around can give insight to the hearts and minds of the people who once turned their pages. It's important to reflect on our past, and where we've come from, and sometimes the best and simplest way to examine that is by looking at exactly what it is that we leave behind us.

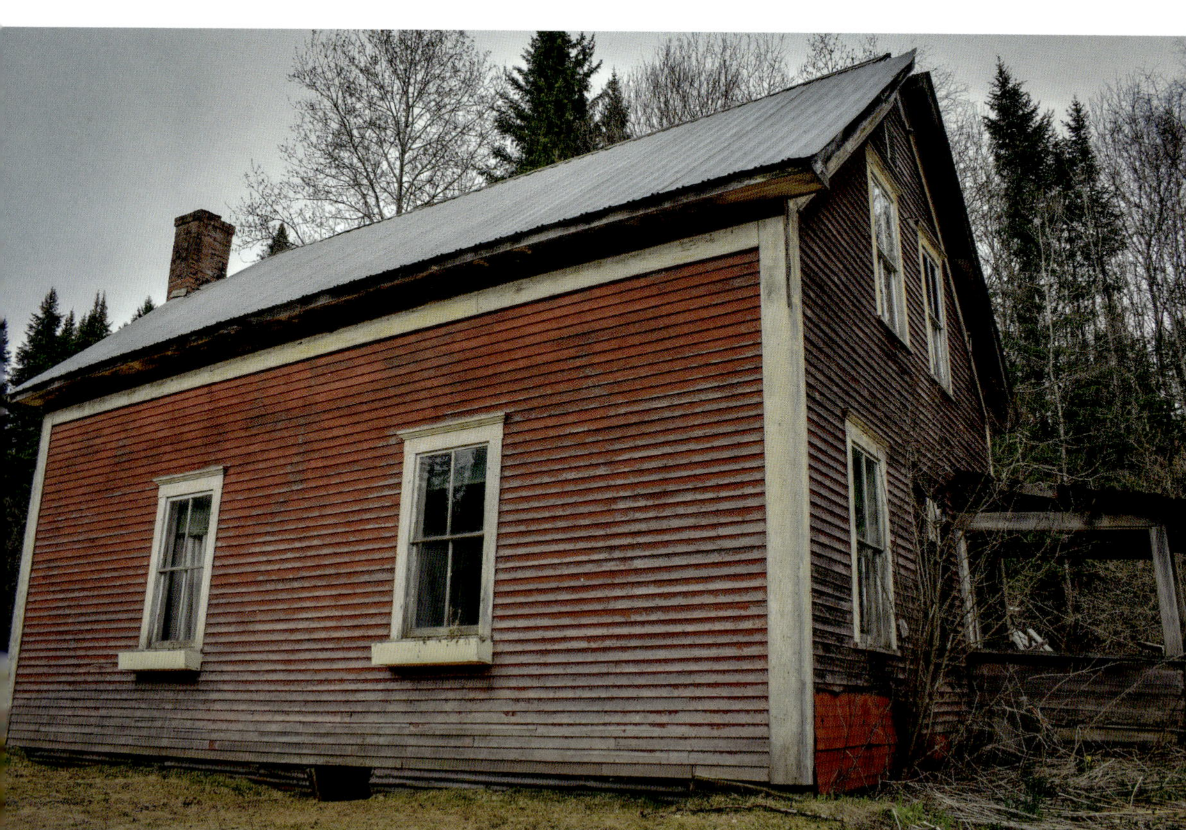

Once used as a schoolhouse and then a private residence for a little while. It has since been torn down.

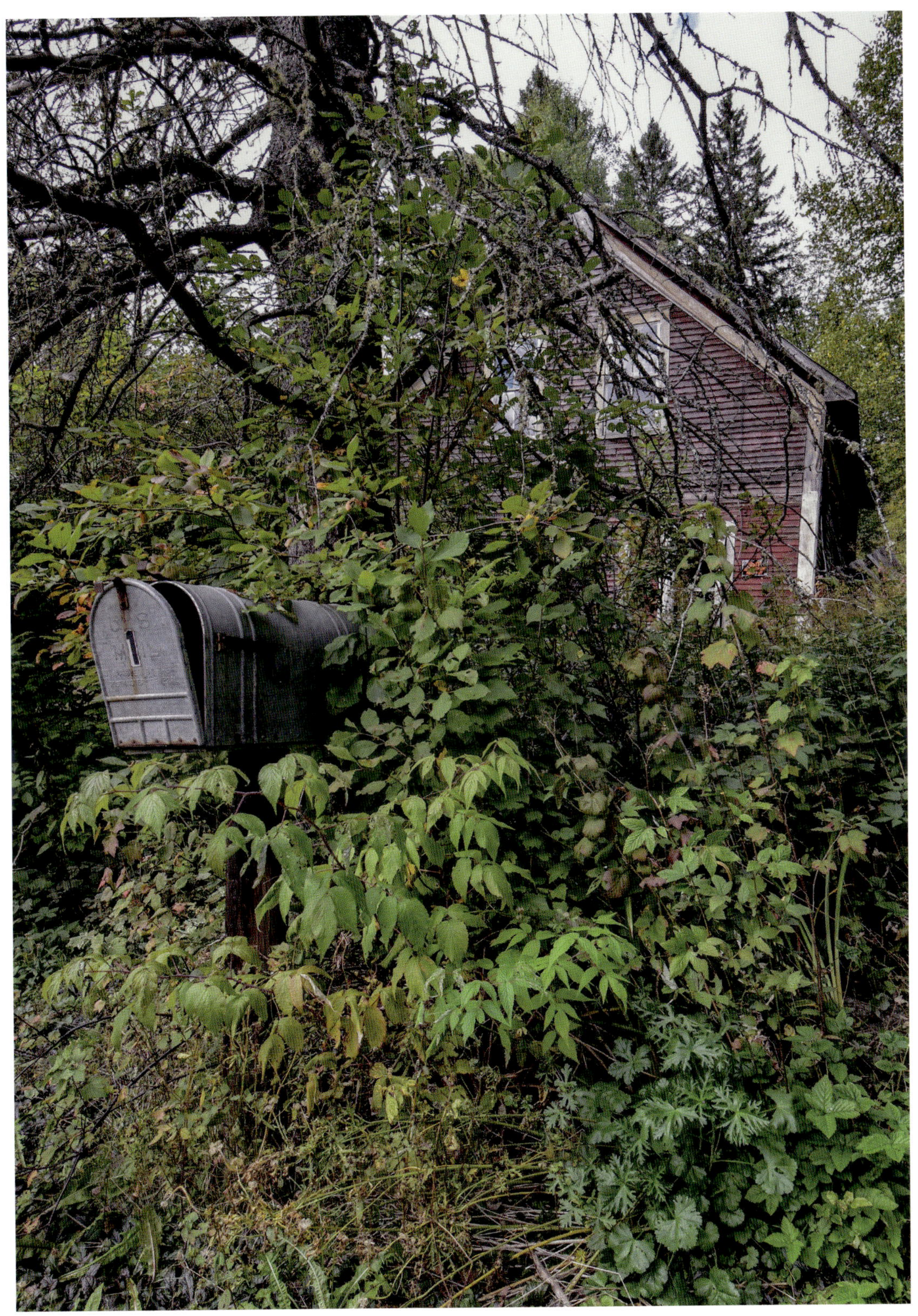

Old schoolhouse and residence.

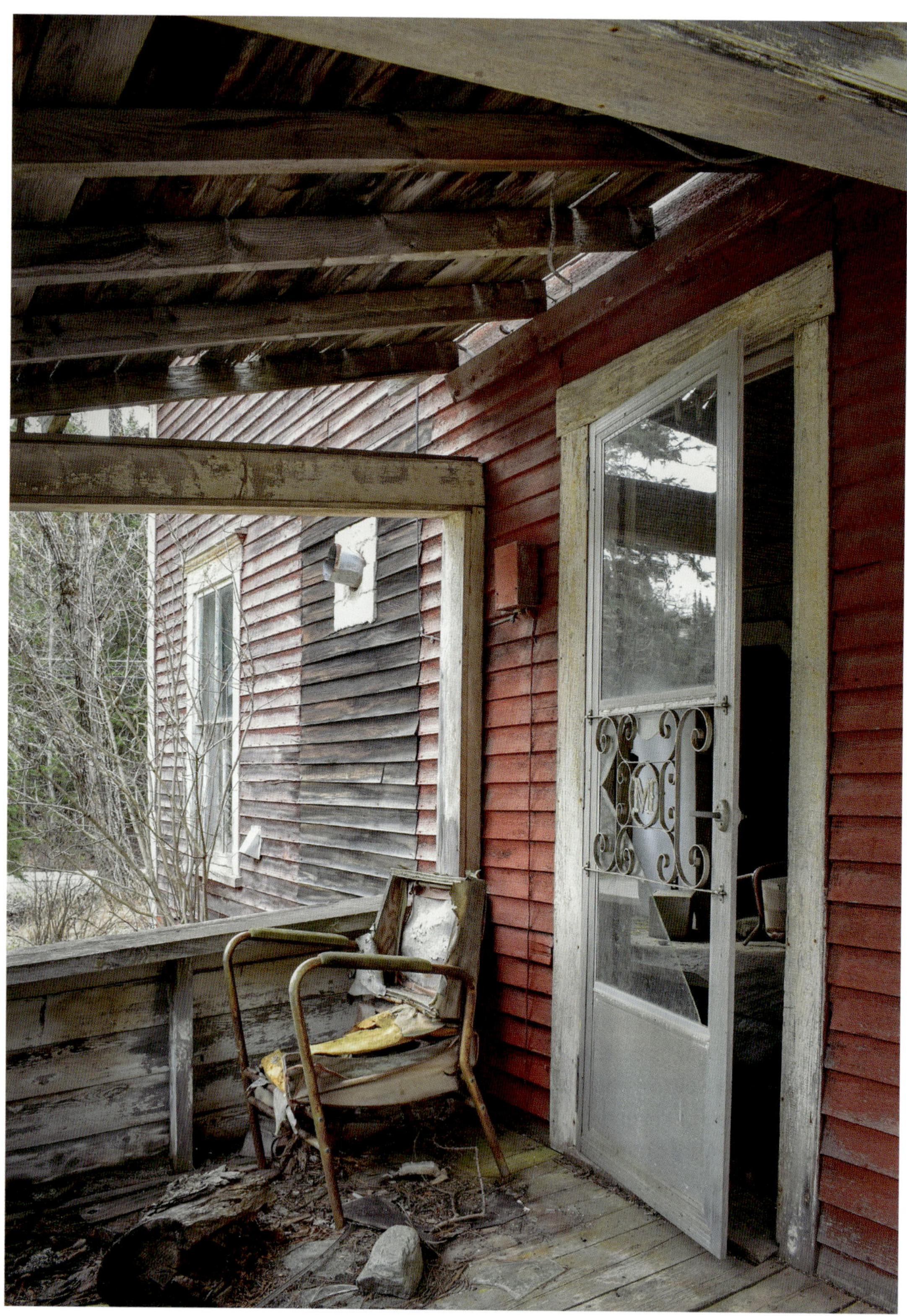

The chair hasn't seen a visitor in a long time.

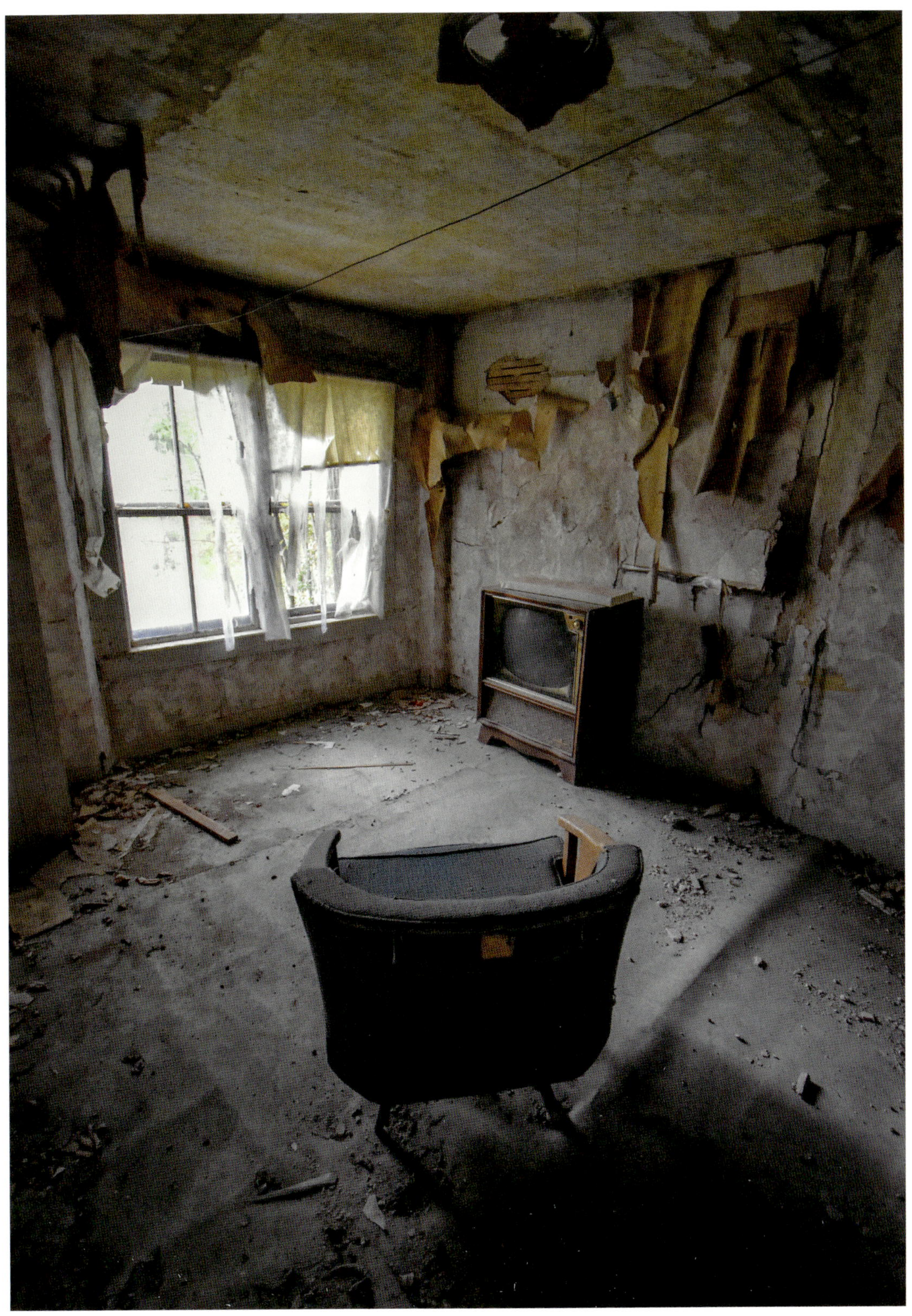

Nothing on TV.

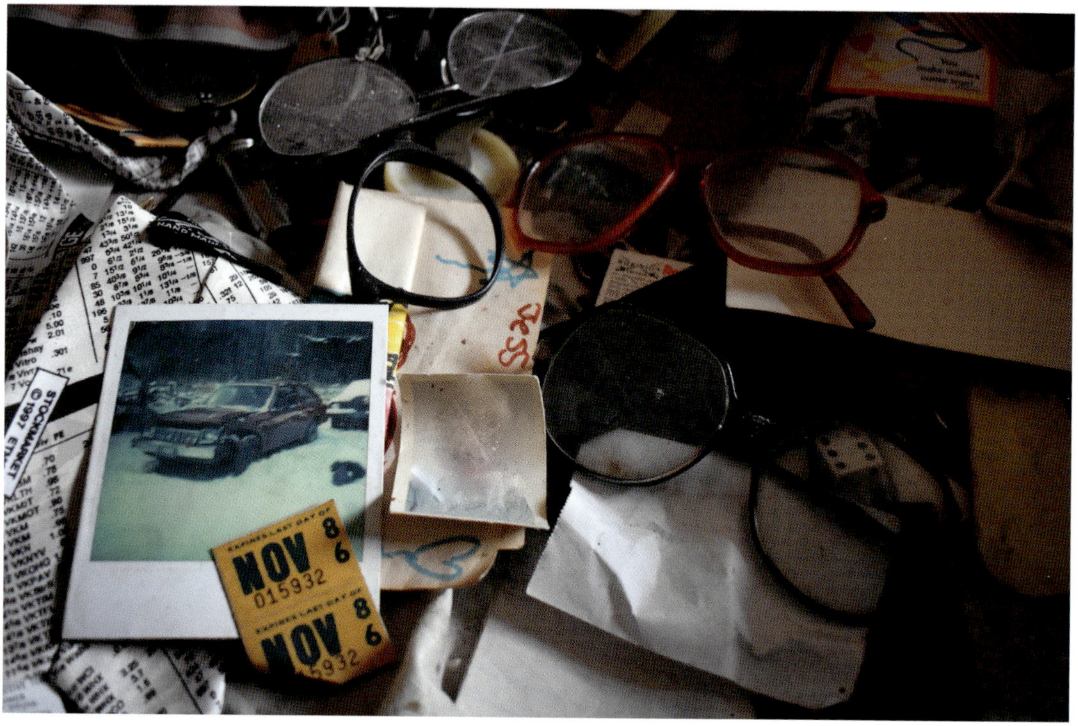

Above: Forgotten photos and mementos from another time.

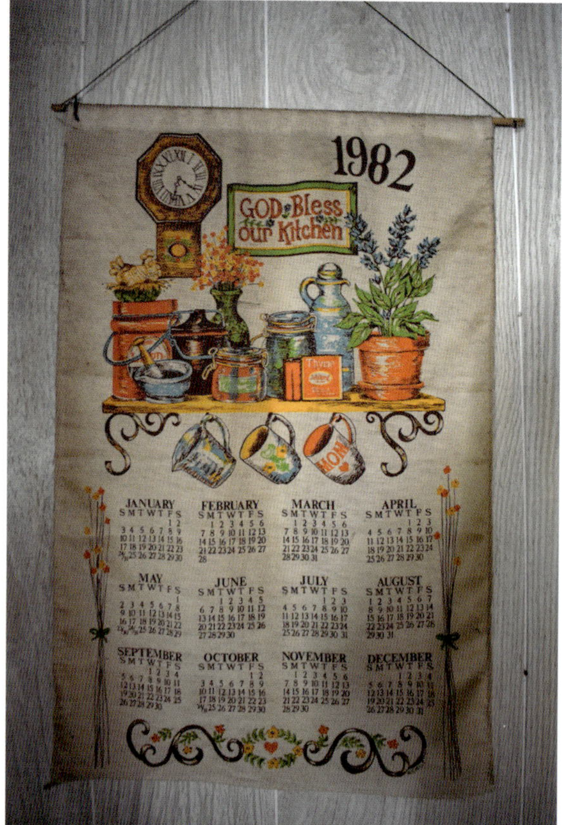

Left: Old calendar from 1982 still hanging on the wall.

Opposite page: What remained of an abandoned farmhouse before it was torn down.

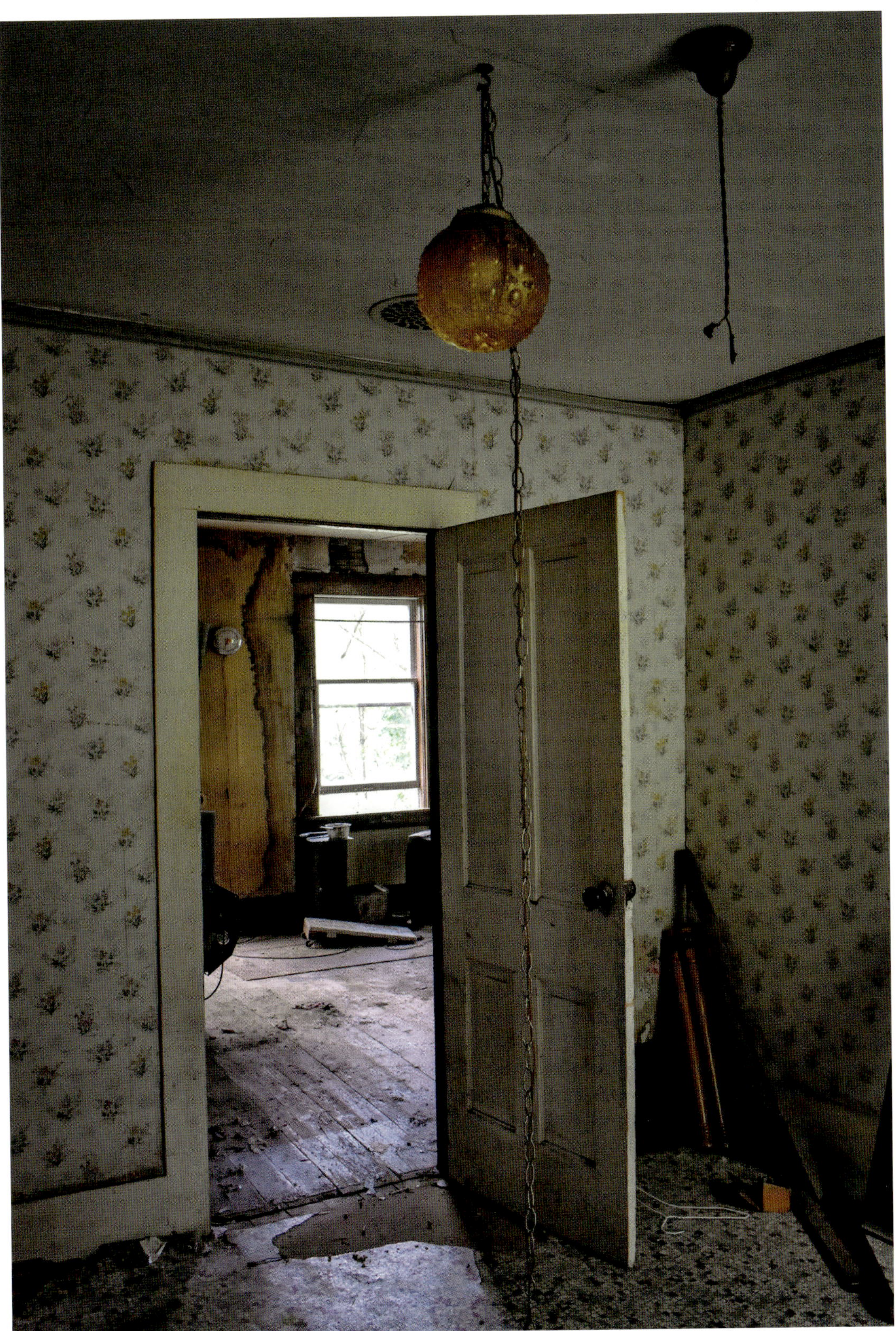

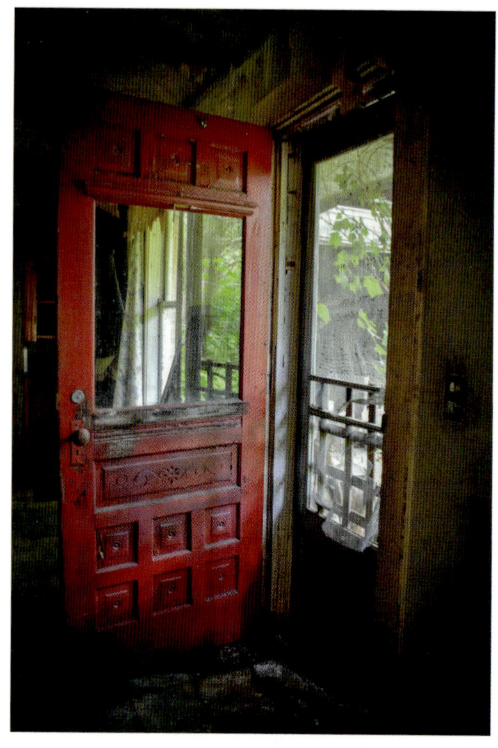

Left: This red door used to welcome guests.

Below: Left behind furniture.

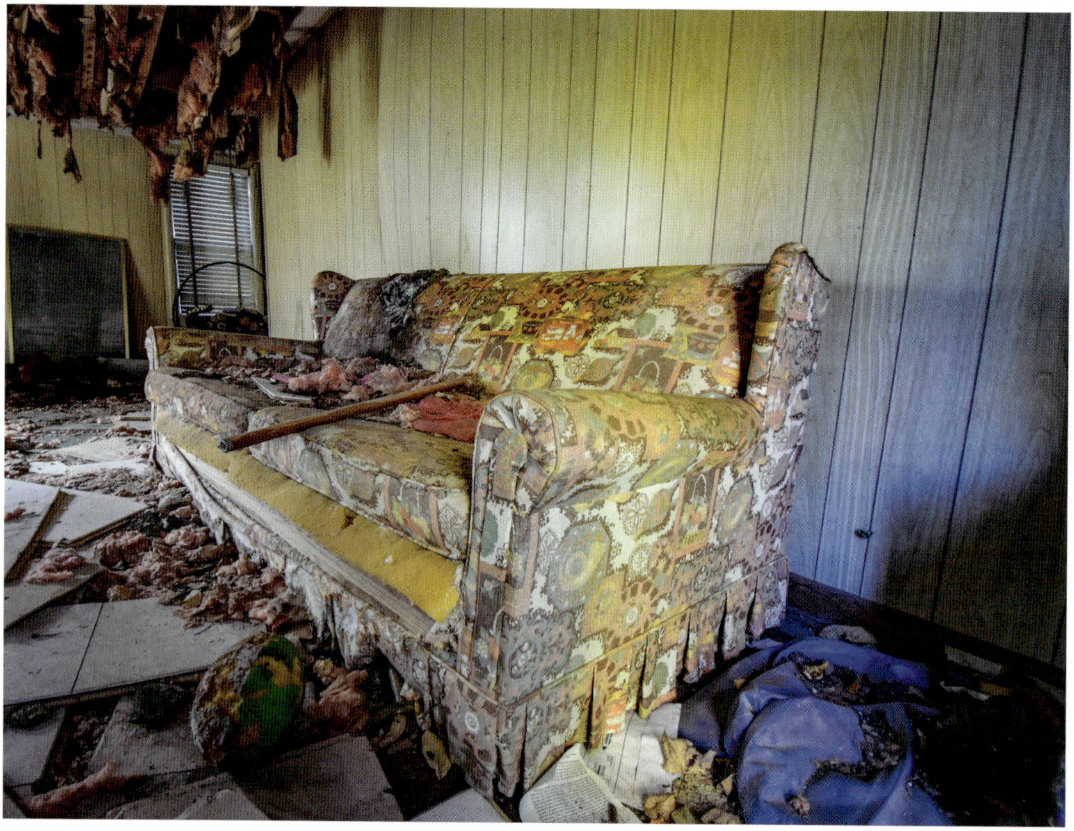

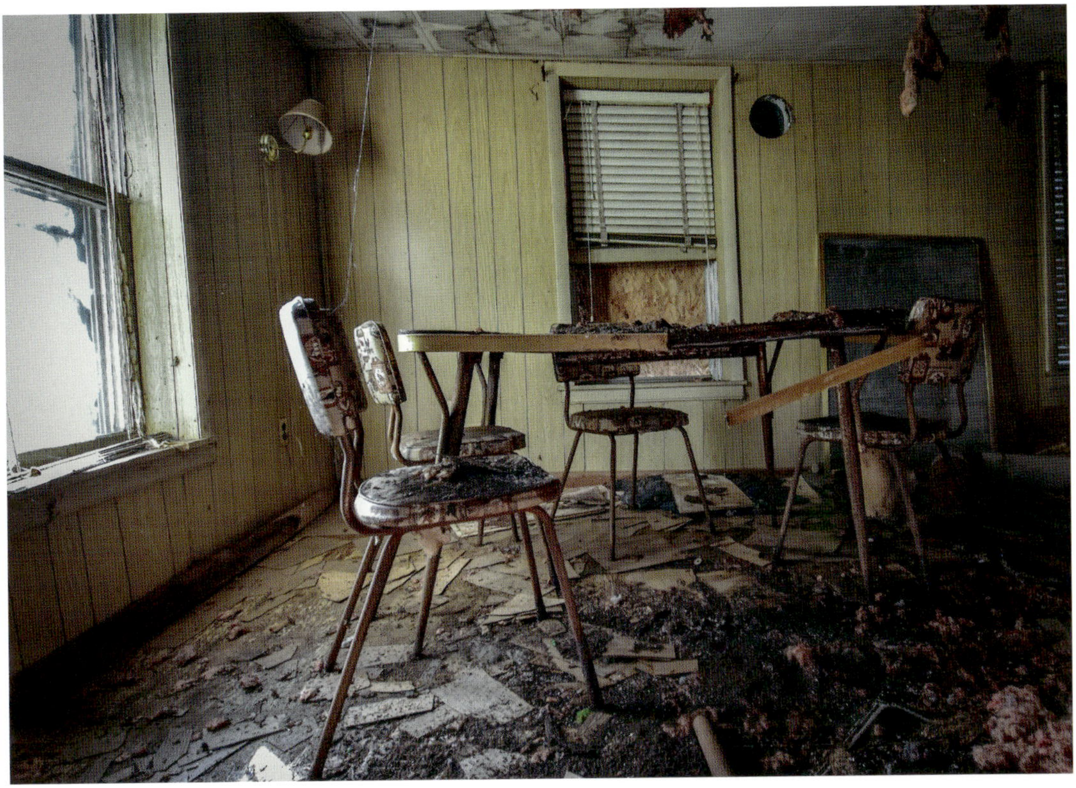

Above: How many family dinners were had at this table?

Right: Once someone's favorite chair.

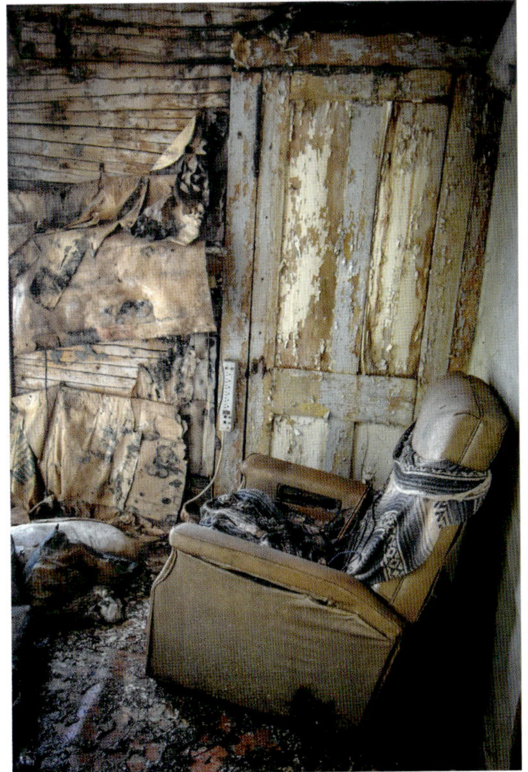

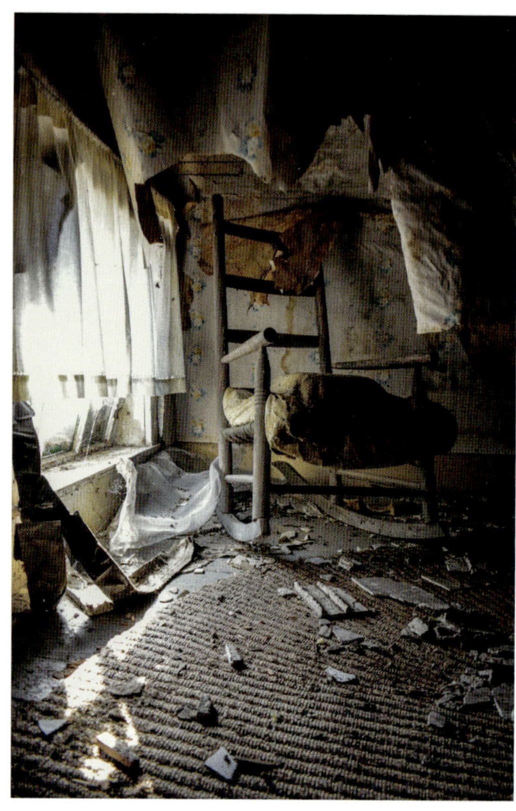

Left: This rocking chair was left behind, next to a bedroom with a baby crib. Was a baby once rocked to sleep here?

Below left: Forgotten technology.

Below right: A built-in cubby holding moldy books and puzzles.

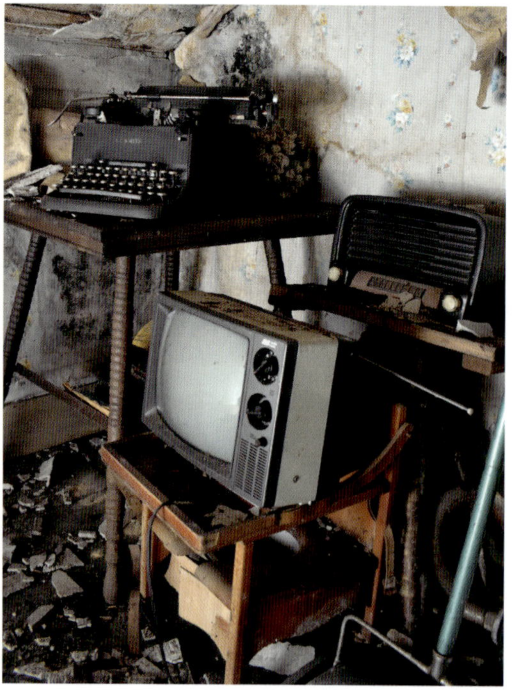

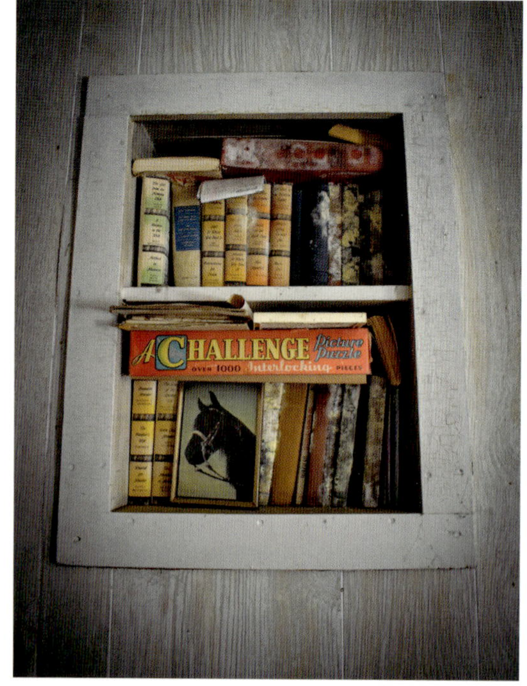

Driving around aimlessly will eventually bring you to areas that may look a little more rundown or neglected than others. Perhaps areas that have been hit harder by tragedy or poverty. Sometimes you'll stumble upon stretches of road that hold more abandonment than you'd expect for an area. I'm sure many of you have driven through the countryside, on roads surrounded on both sides by seemingly endless hay fields, with a scattering of abandoned barns. Many of you have probably driven past an abandoned house, and perhaps even wondered about its history.

In the fall, when the leaves begin to change and the morning air is crisp, it ushers in a swift reminder of the cold, snowy winter days soon to come. One beautiful homestead has managed to withstand over a century and a half of those cold, snowy days. The house was built in 1854 by B. A. Rolfe of Groveton. In 1909, Mary and Archie Stills sold the homestead to George and Carrie Nevers of East Lancaster. It was there, in what became known as The Nevers' Homestead, that they raised their seven children. As was common during that time, the family supplemented their income by renting rooms and providing meals. The house, once full of family and guests, now sits abandoned with breathtaking views being quickly taken over by ivy.

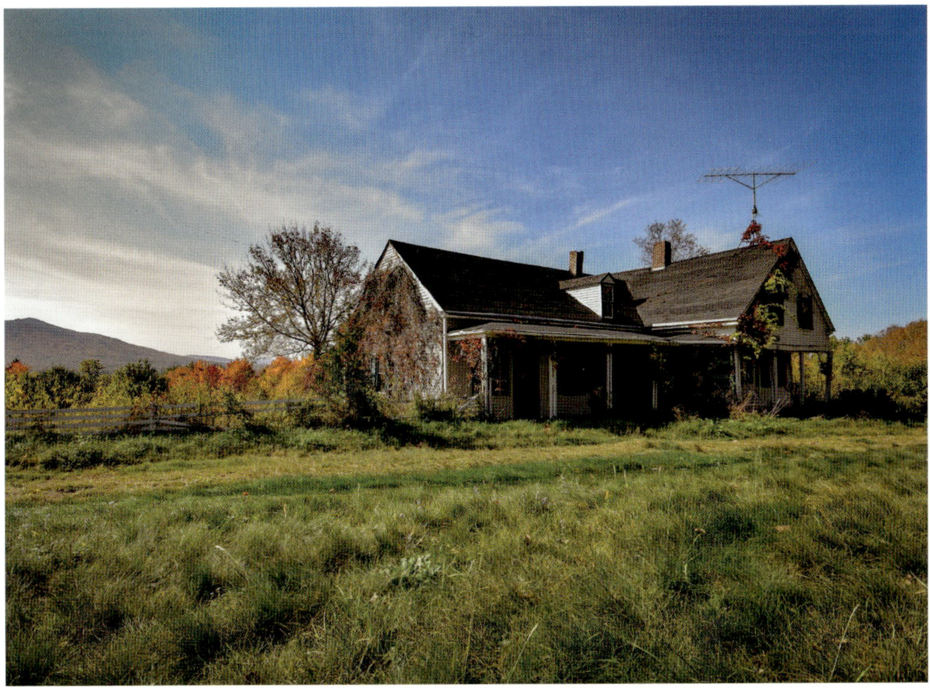

The Nevers' homestead as it stands today.

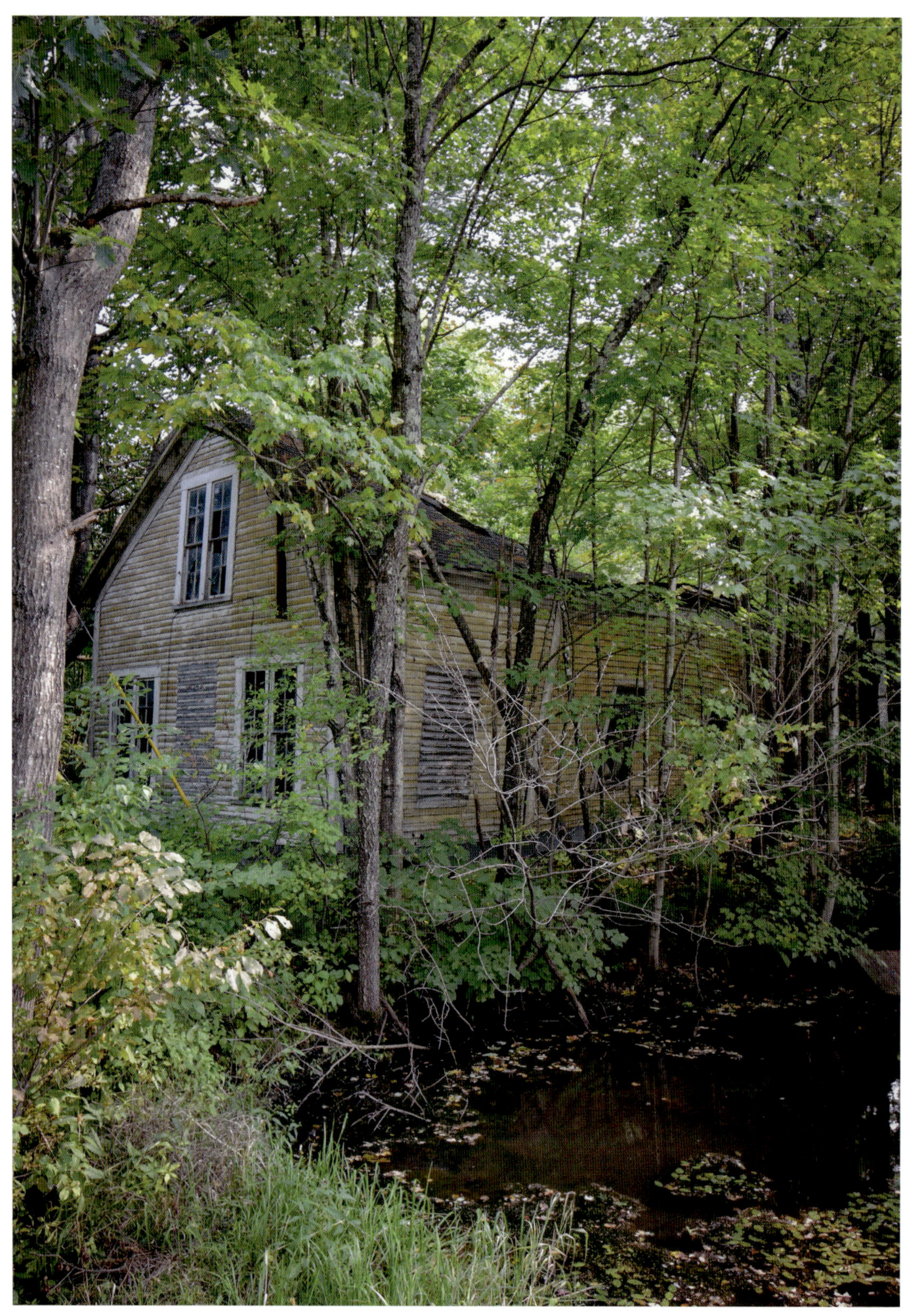

Abandoned alongside a small pond.

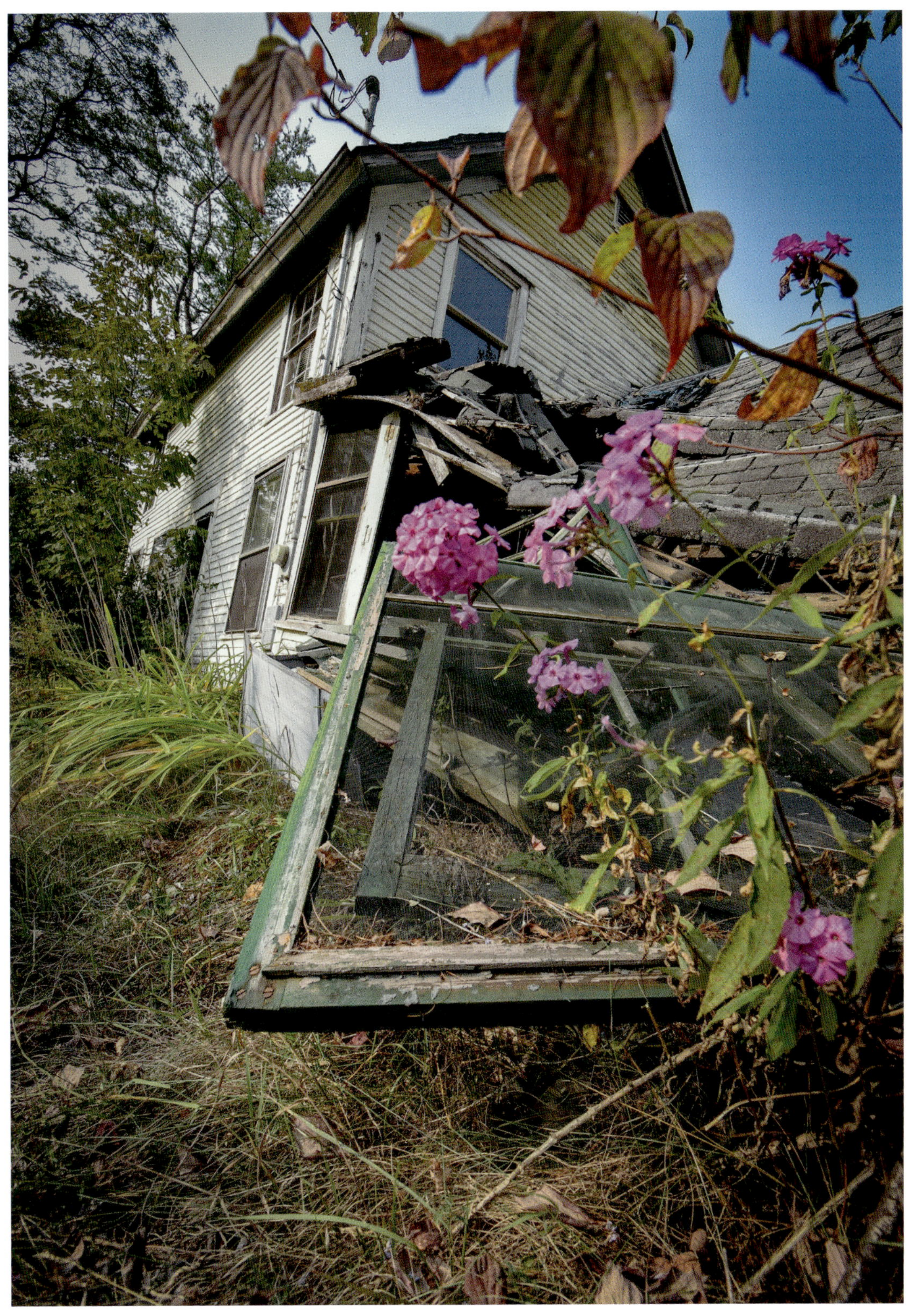

The porch had almost completely collapsed when I came across this house.

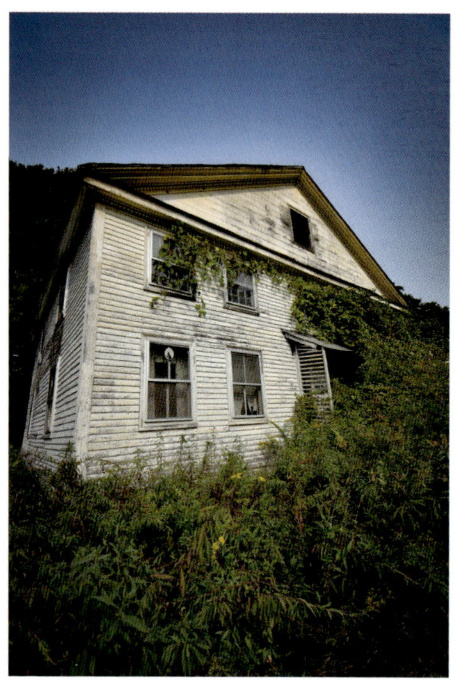

When I was younger, I'd often see these "Tot Finder" stickers in windows.

I used to believe that houses were only a part of our histories and our stories, but lately I've started looking at it differently. Though these places are a part of our histories, we are just as much a part of theirs. Many houses will see people come and go, and we all eventually become chapters in the stories that make these spaces what they are. From the pencil-drawn height charts scratched into the side of doorframes, with coinciding names or years, to the handpicked, peeling wallpaper and left behind house keys that will never be used again, houses have a way of holding on to bits of history. Sometimes I'll come across places or things that remind me of parts of my own life, and for a minute I will share in the discarded nostalgia.

A home built in the mid-1800s by Edward Merrill for his son, Daniel, and his wife, Caroline, may be one of the most photographed abandoned houses in northern New Hampshire. Daniel's son, Charles, and Charles' wife, Eva, lived here years later with their two children. Of those children, eventually Fay, their son, returned to the house in his adulthood in the 1920s with his wife and three children. Eventually, they also left this house behind, and it was used as a rental property, mostly for family. The house was last occupied around 2000. I wouldn't say that this place has been lonely, considering the large number of people who seek it out to get a glance of the house that has been put through years of harsh northern New Hampshire winters and somehow still manages to stand. It's a true testament to craftsmanship of the past.

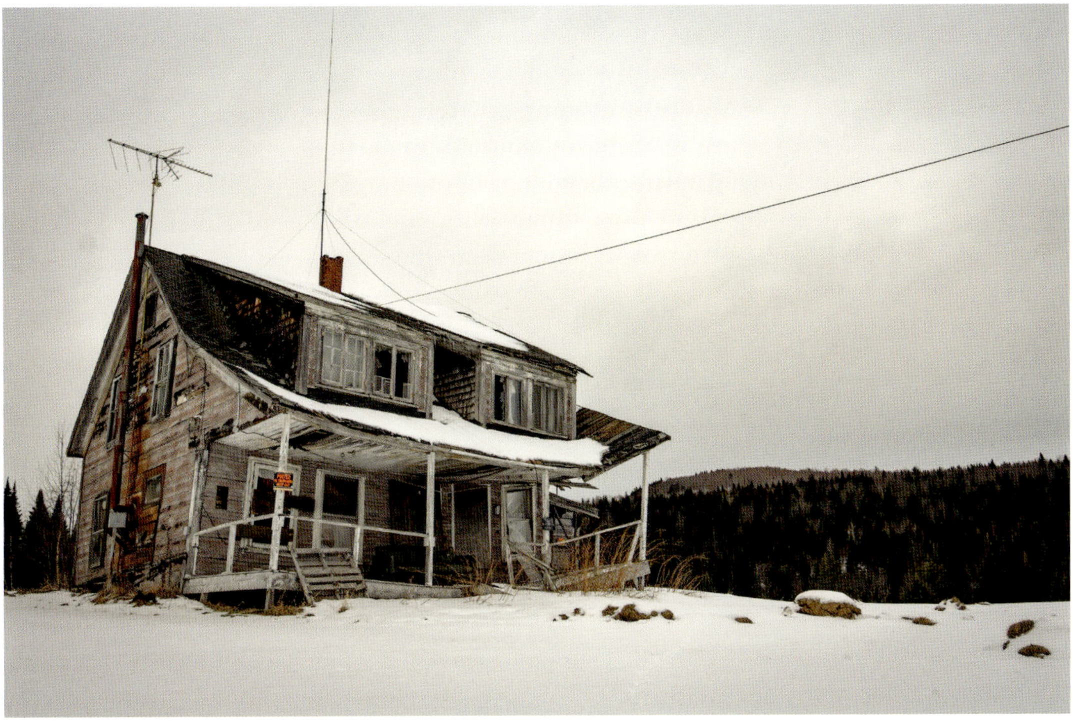

The old Merrill farm in northern New Hampshire.

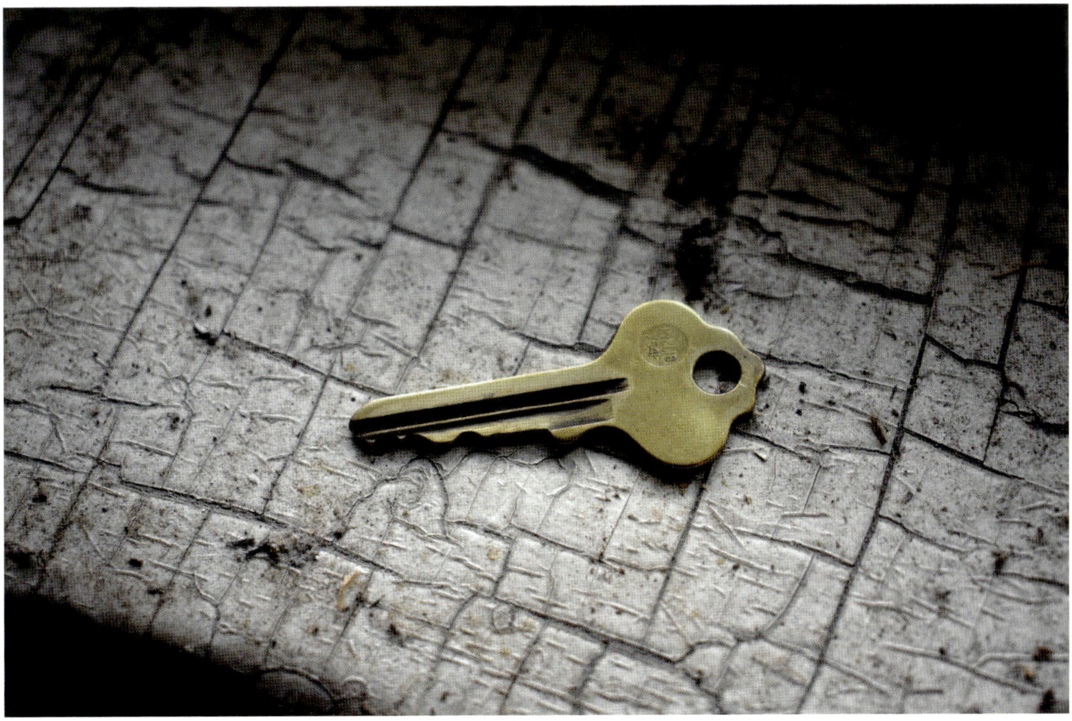

Left behind house key on a dusty windowsill.

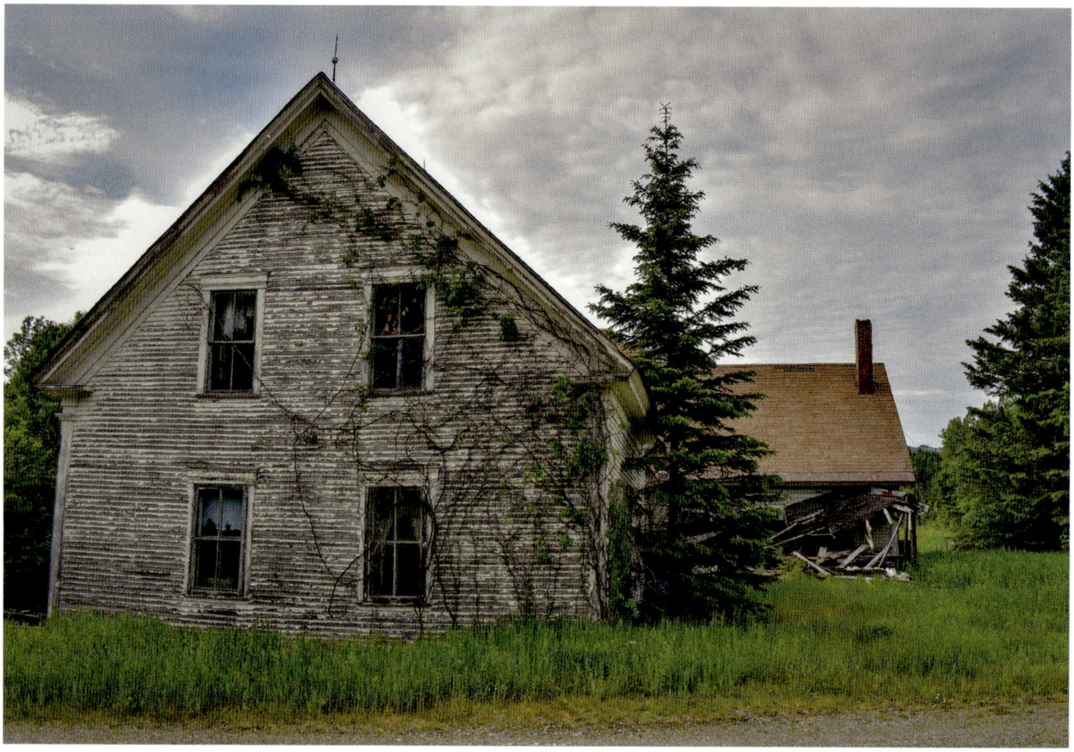

Abandoned farmstead on a dirt road in northern New Hampshire.

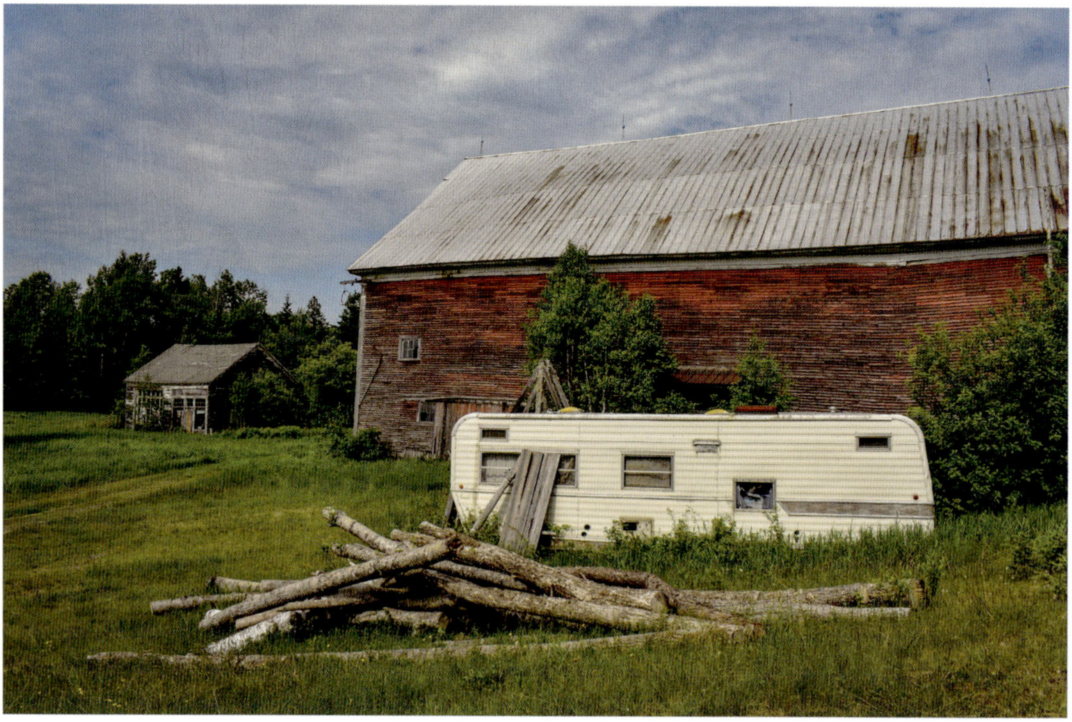

Abandoned farmstead barn.

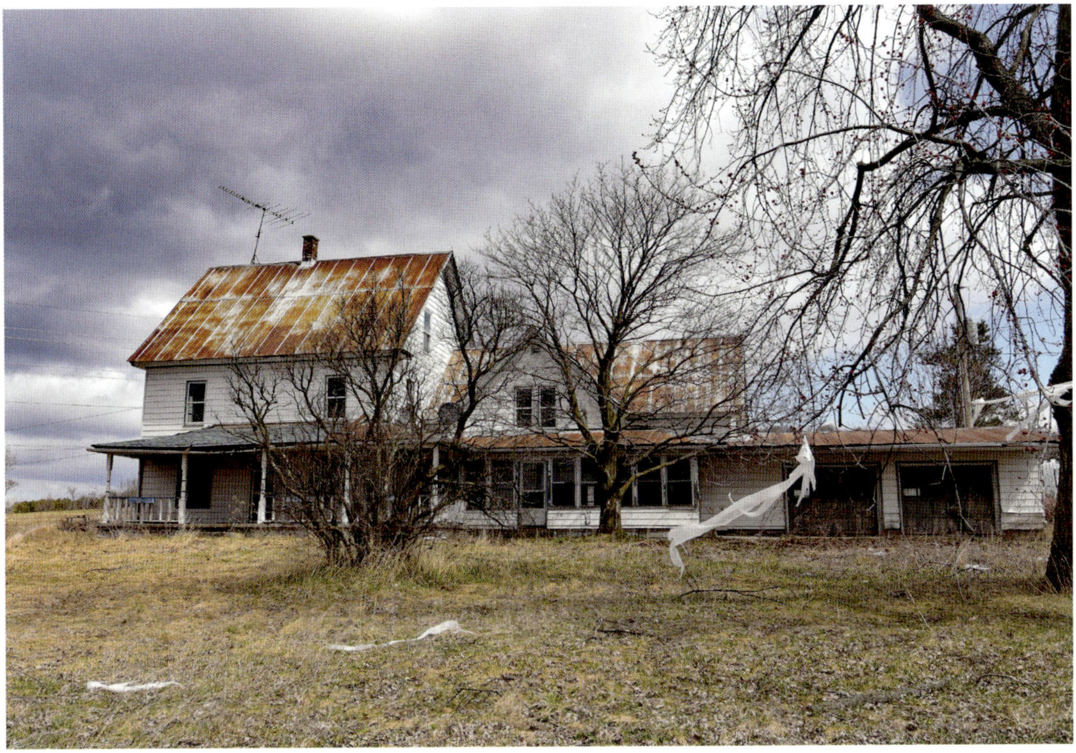

There is something a little haunting about the hay bale wrapping that is caught and blowing in the tree branches.

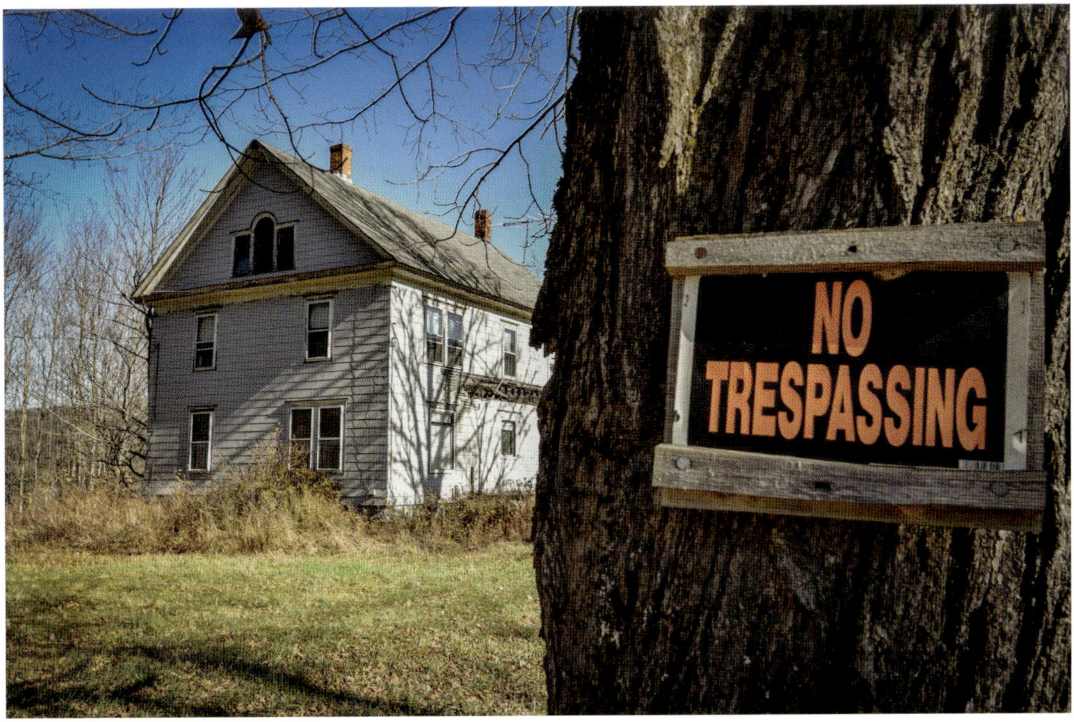

Hiding behind the signs.

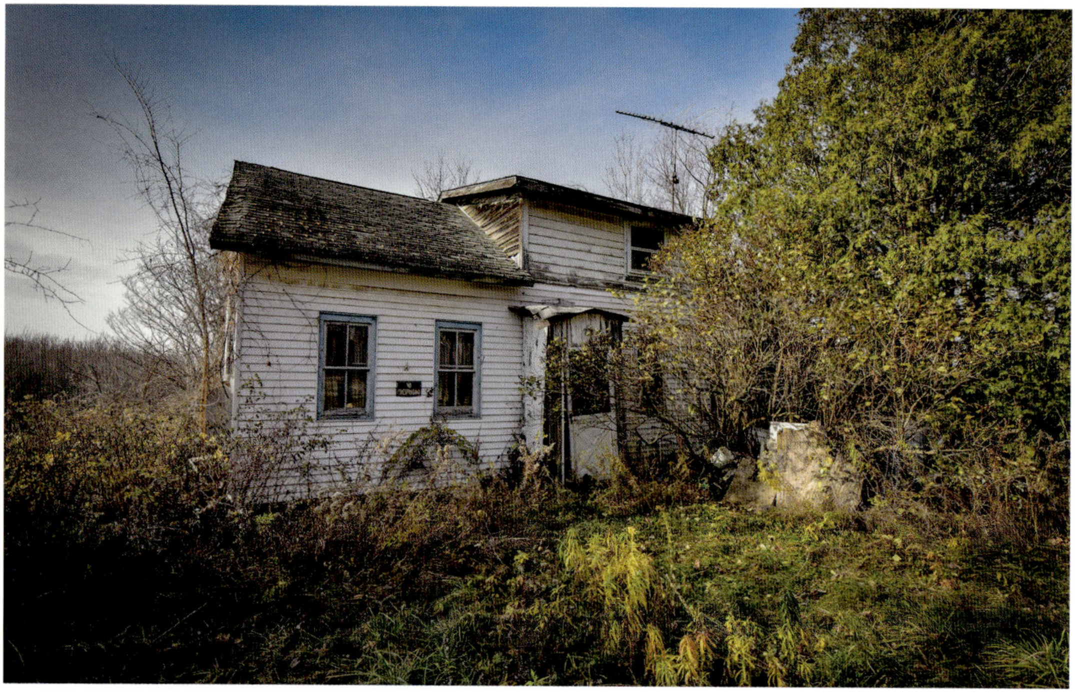

Hidden behind the trees.

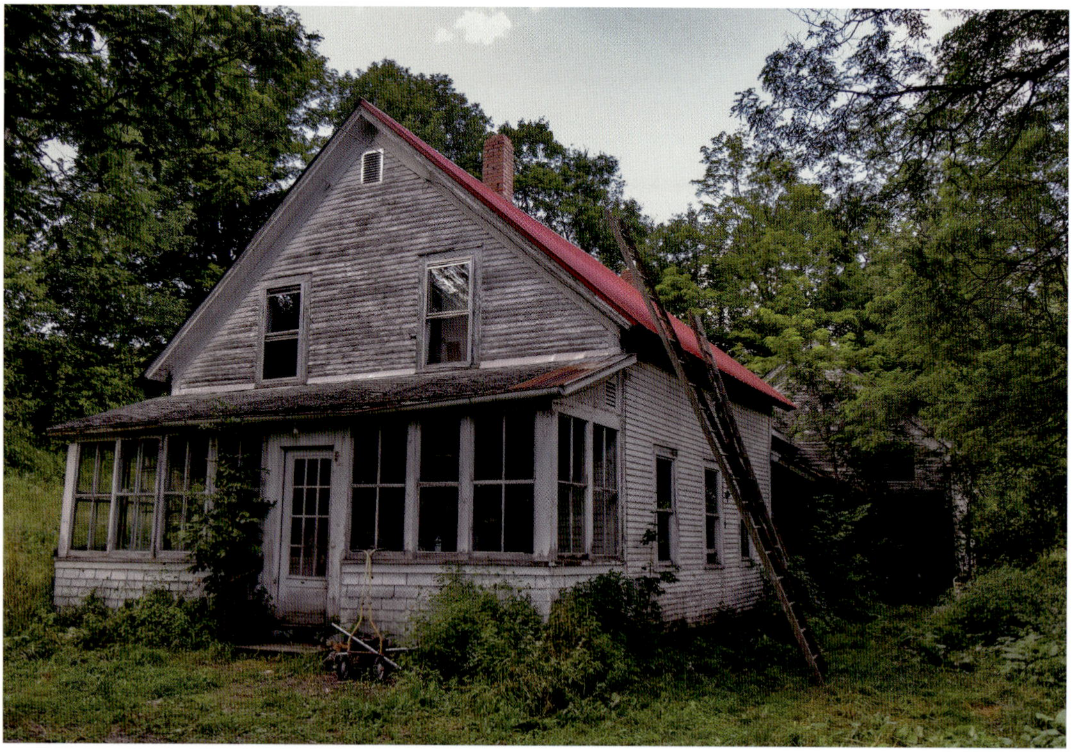

This house has since been torn down, but before it was, there were reminders of those who lived there scattered throughout.

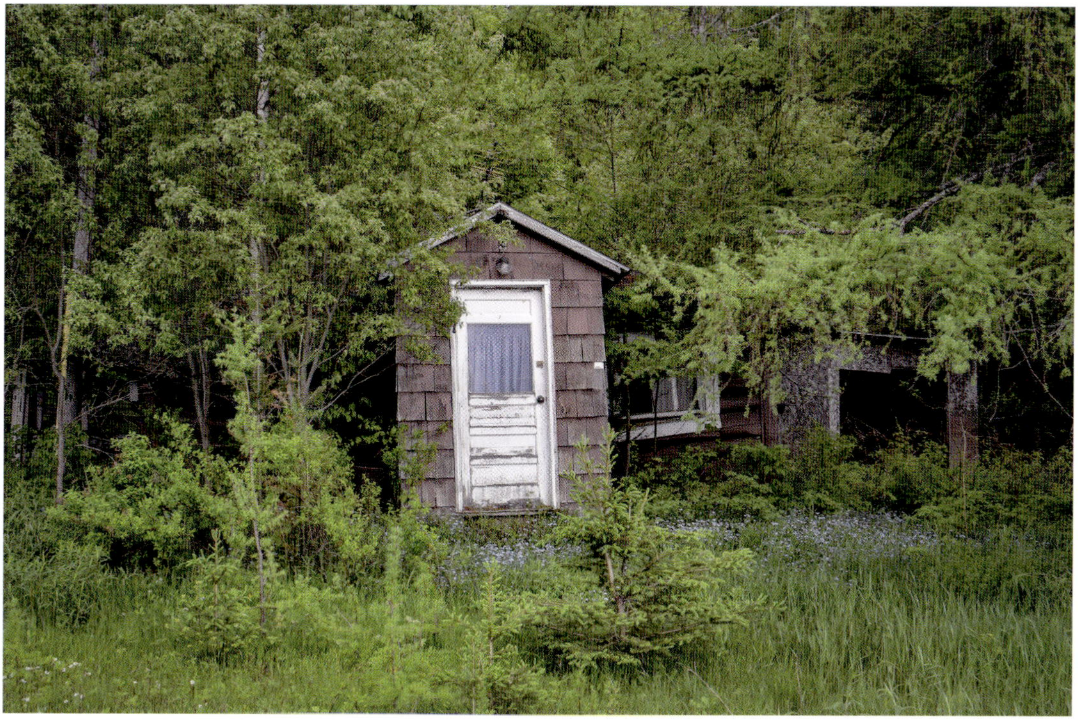

Above: A small camp crumbling behind a wall of flowers and trees.

Right: An unassuming, old farmhouse hidden behind the crabapple trees.

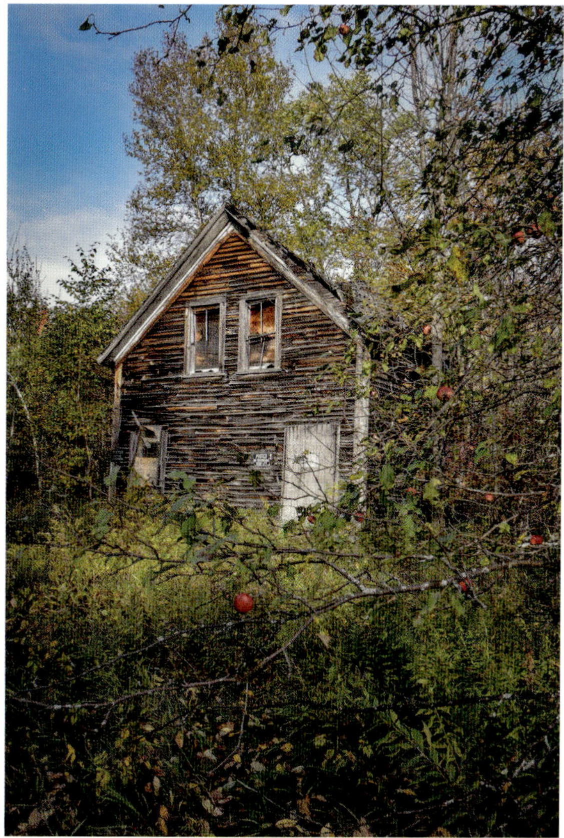

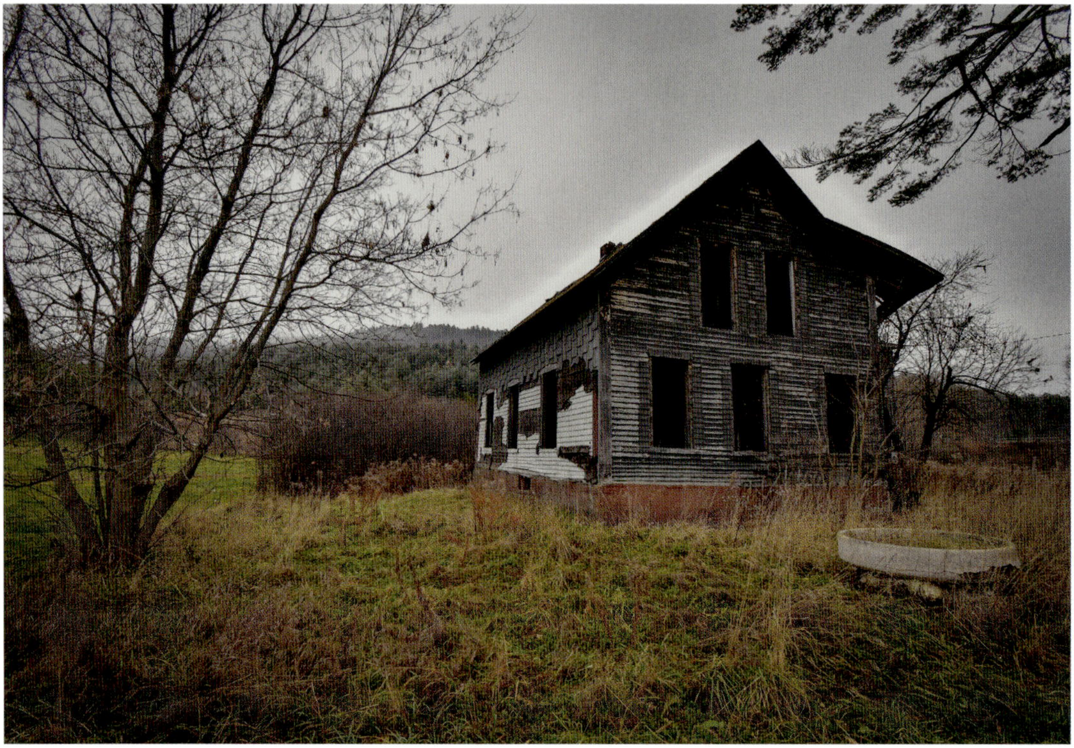

A foggy morning makes abandoned houses look a little more forgotten.

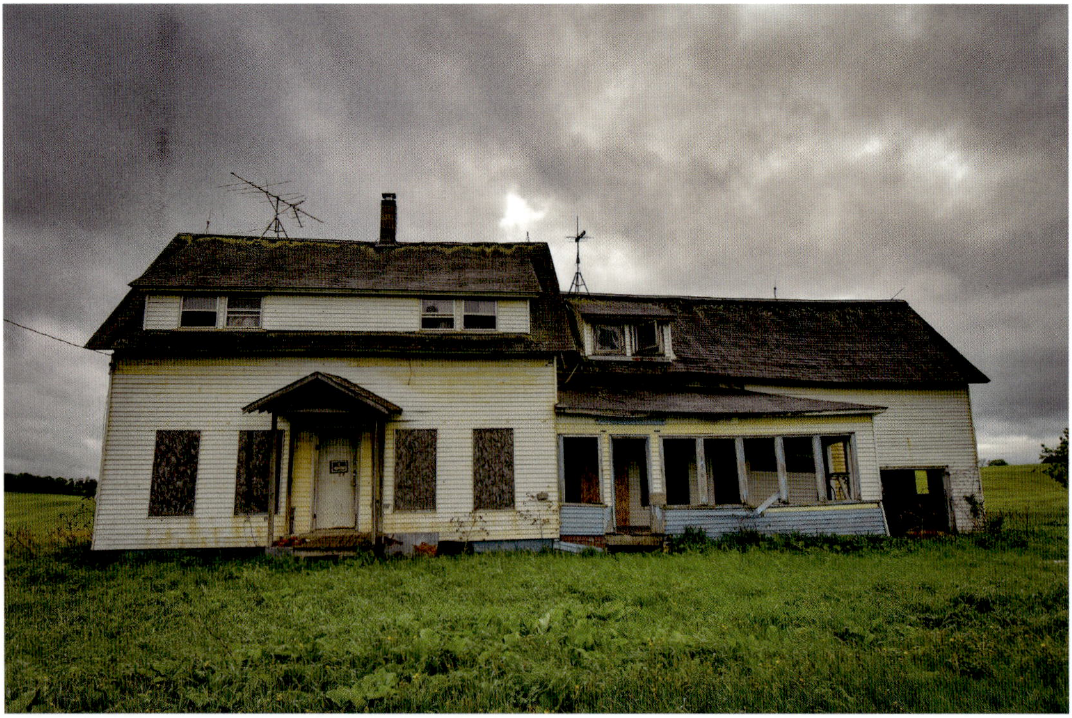

This house recently burned down, but it sat abandoned for years while the land was still being used.

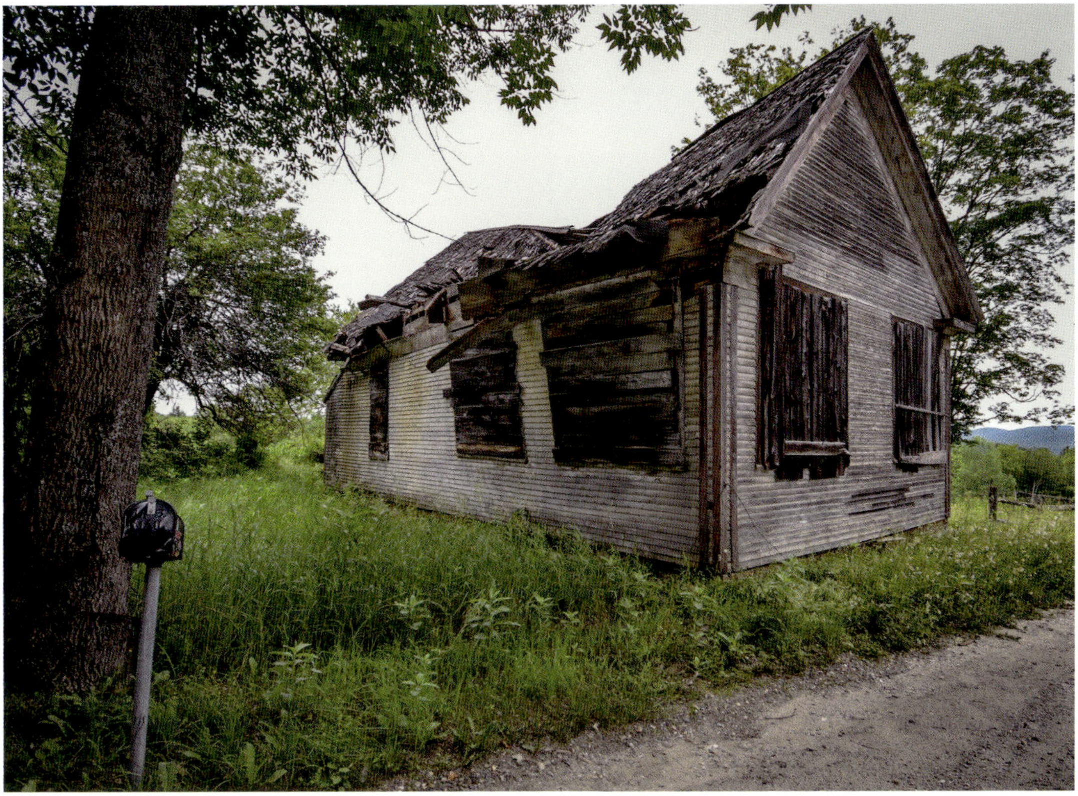

Above: The roof of this abandoned schoolhouse is almost caved in.

Right: Set back from the road, this house sits abandoned, but not empty. There are reminders of those who used to live there left behind.

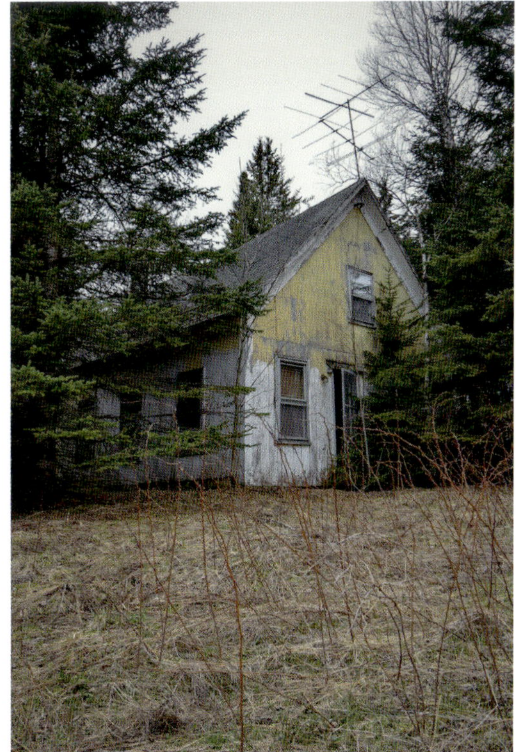

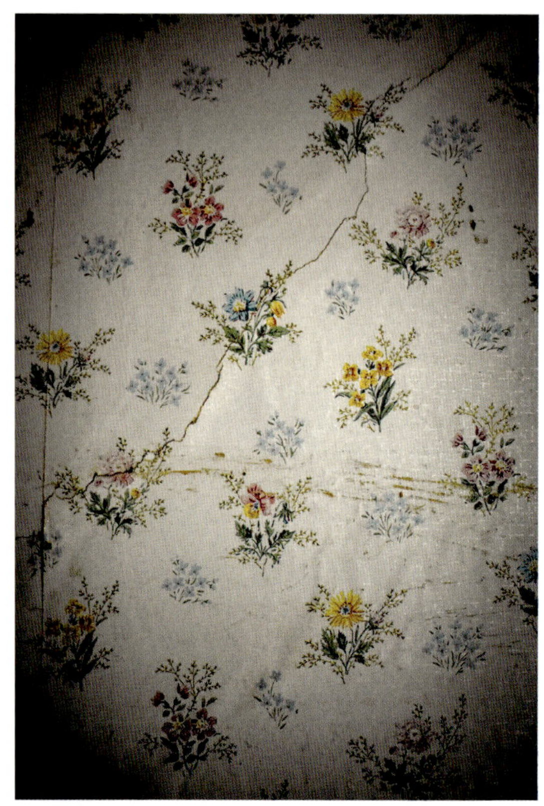

Left: Wallpaper always tells a story of the people who chose it.

Below: On a sprawling country road, this house stands forgotten.

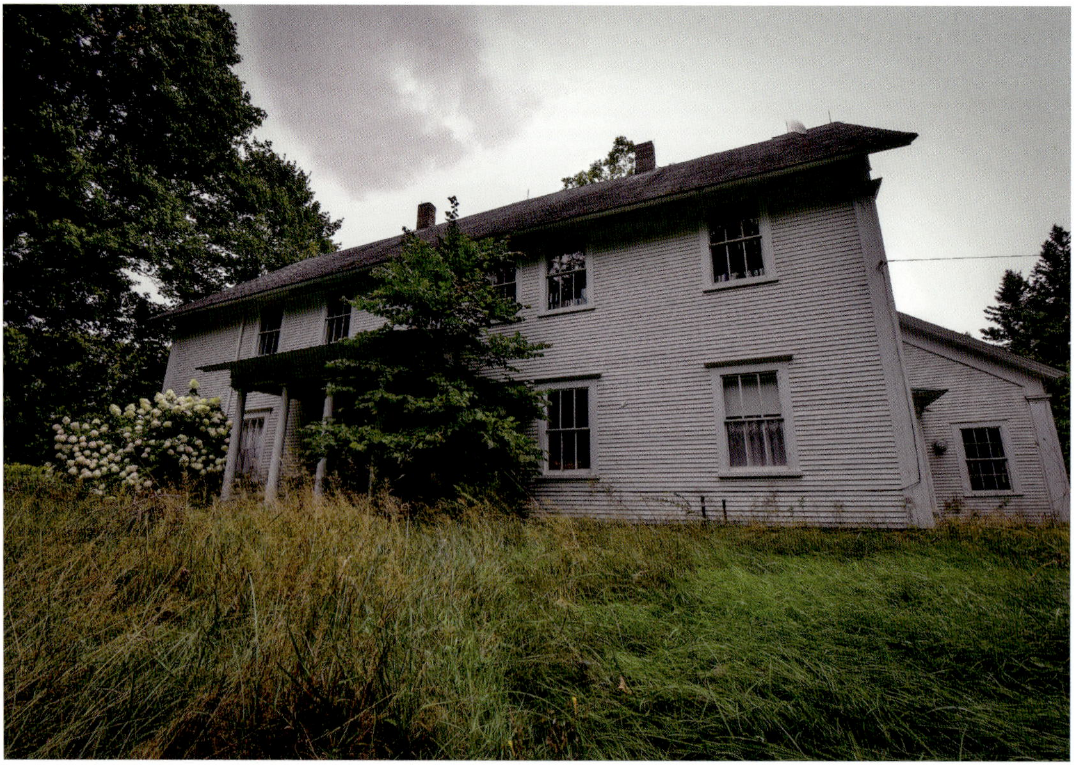

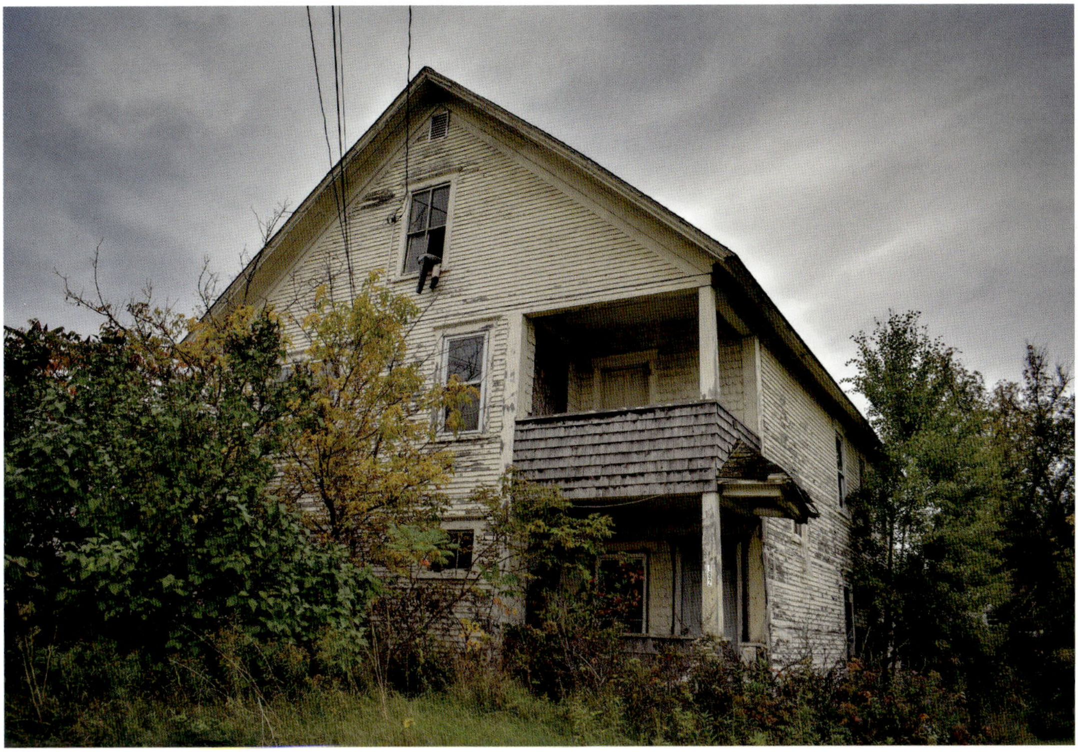

Someone thought it would be funny to leave a doll's legs hanging out of the window.

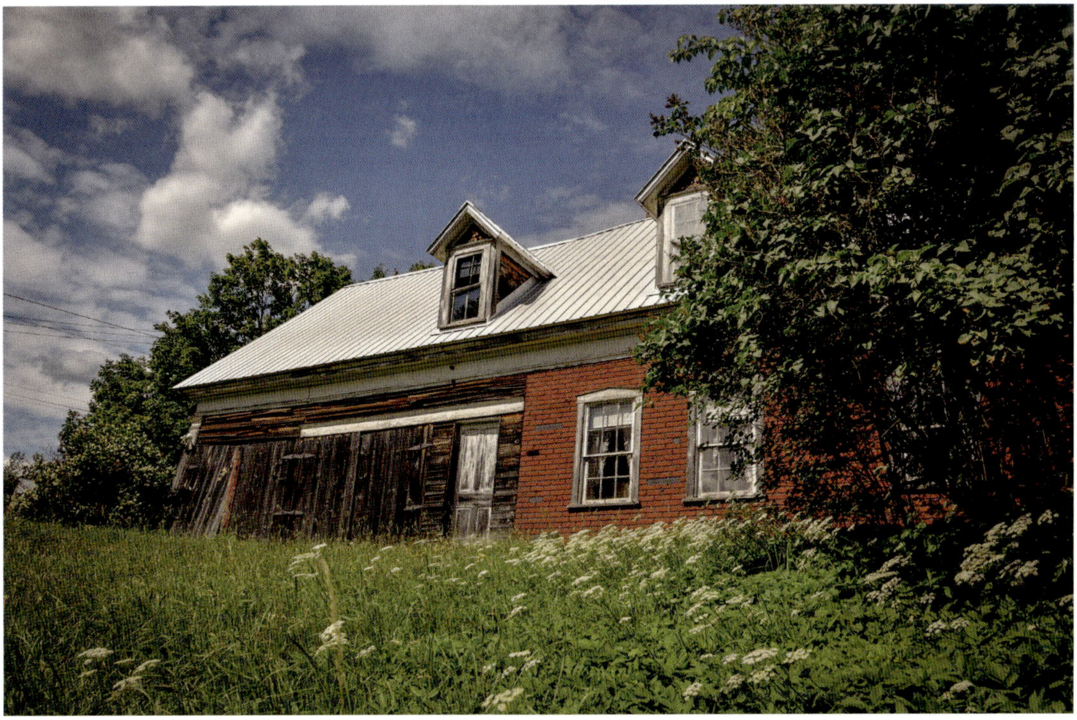

A beautiful, old farmhouse on a dead-end road.

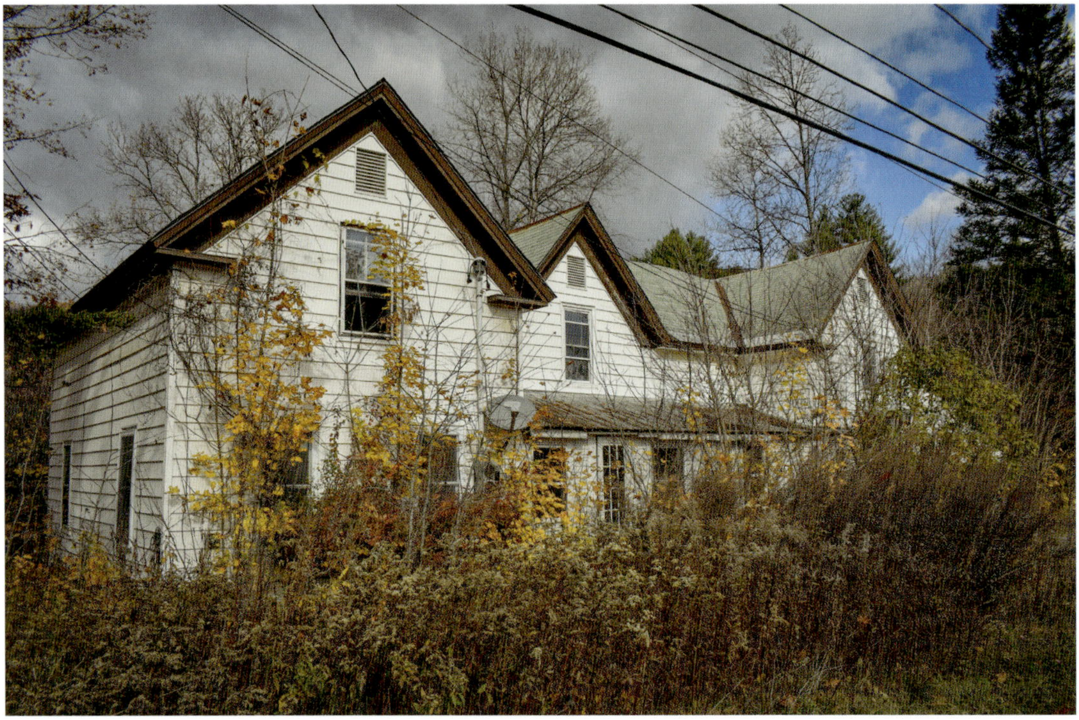

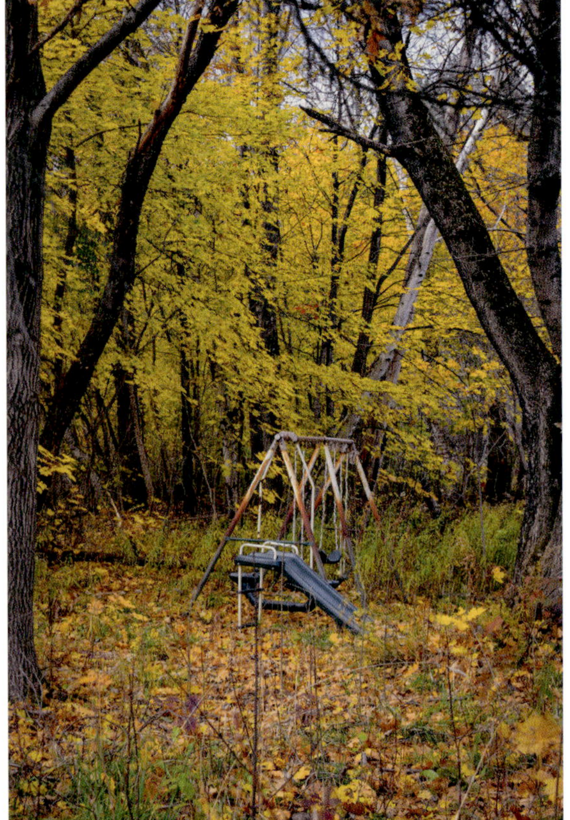

Above: A gutted house on the side of the road.

Left: A left behind swing set.

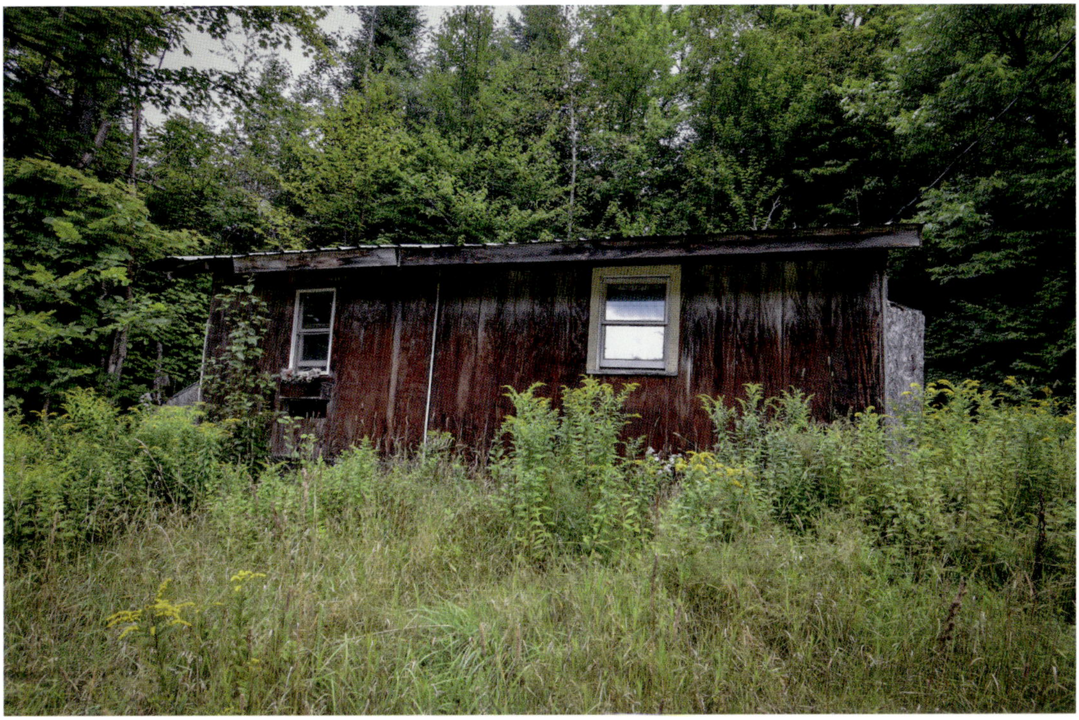

Above: This old camp in New Hampshire once had someone who loved it and left fake flowers in the window boxes.

Right: More peeling wallpaper found in the kitchen of an abandoned house.

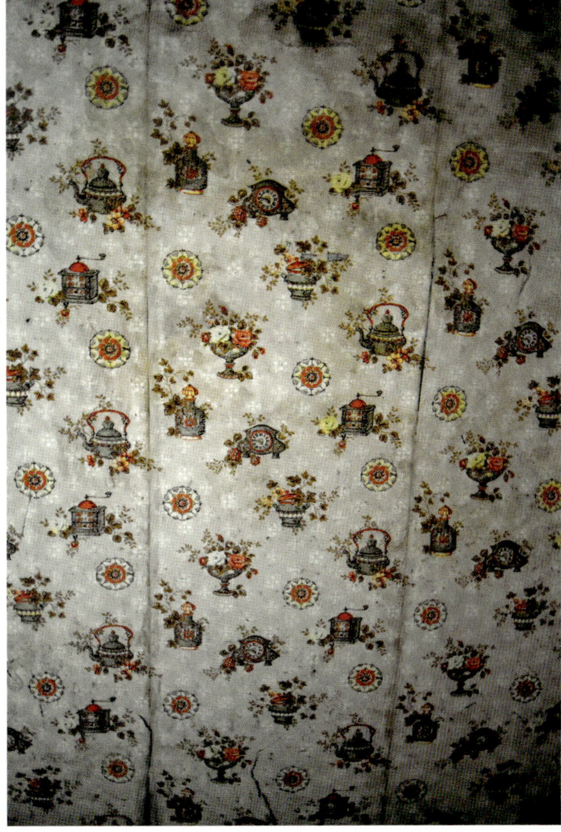

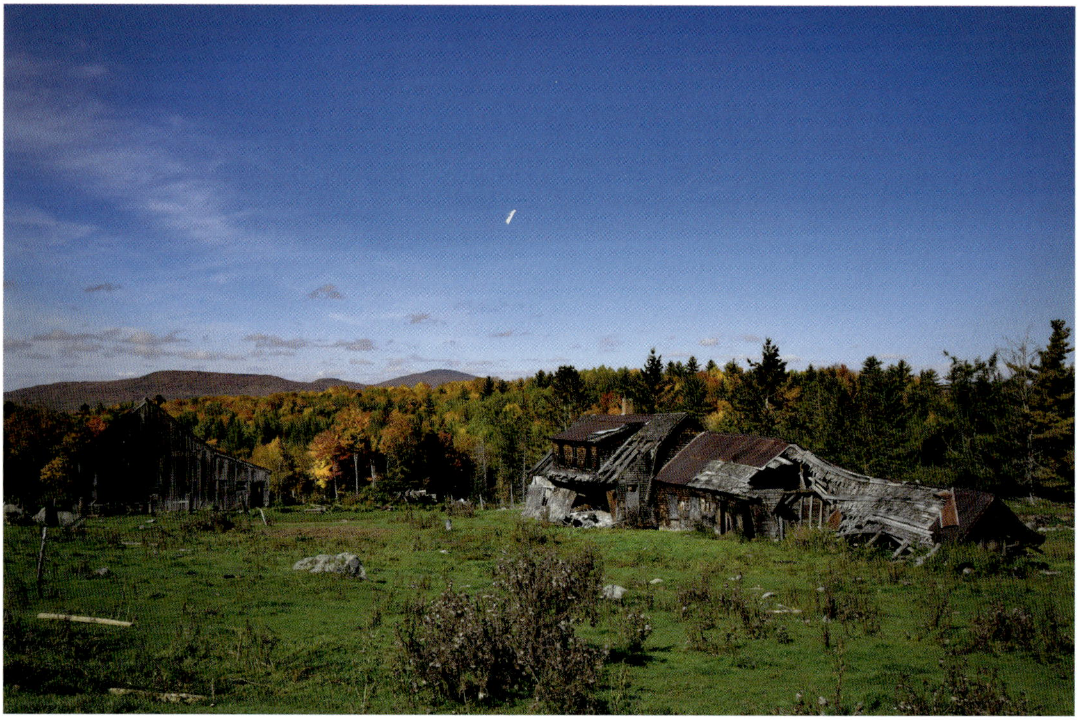

The only residents this New Hampshire farm has left are the cows that graze the fields with beautiful views of the mountains. The house has long since collapsed and is no longer safe for living.

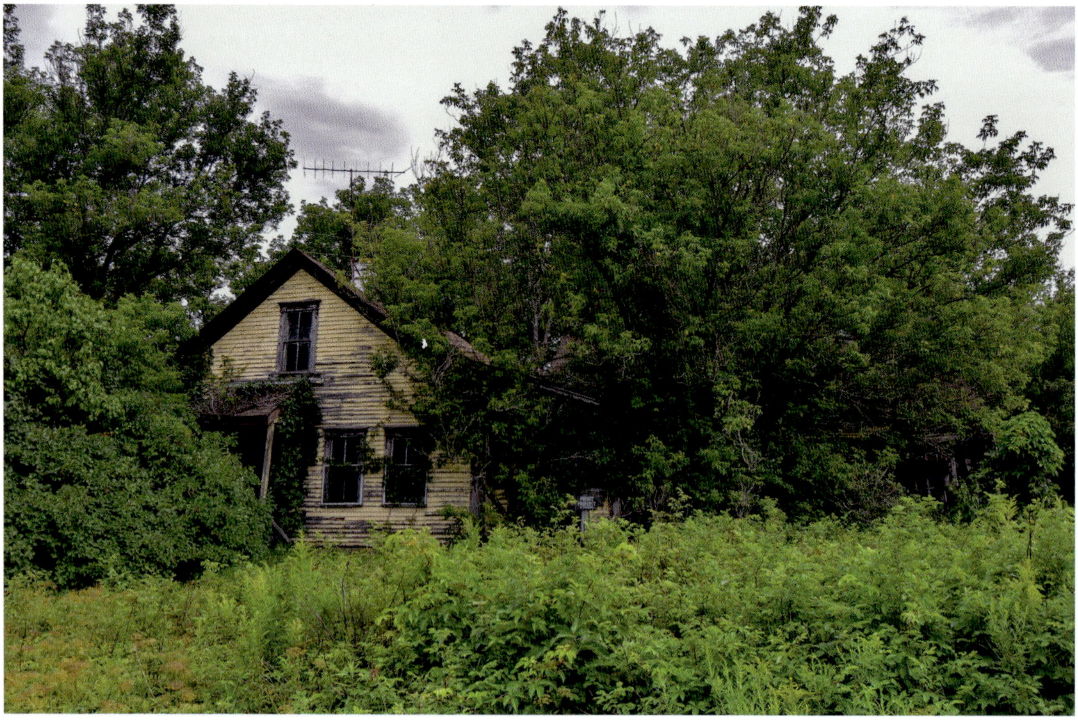

This strip of road has several abandoned houses.

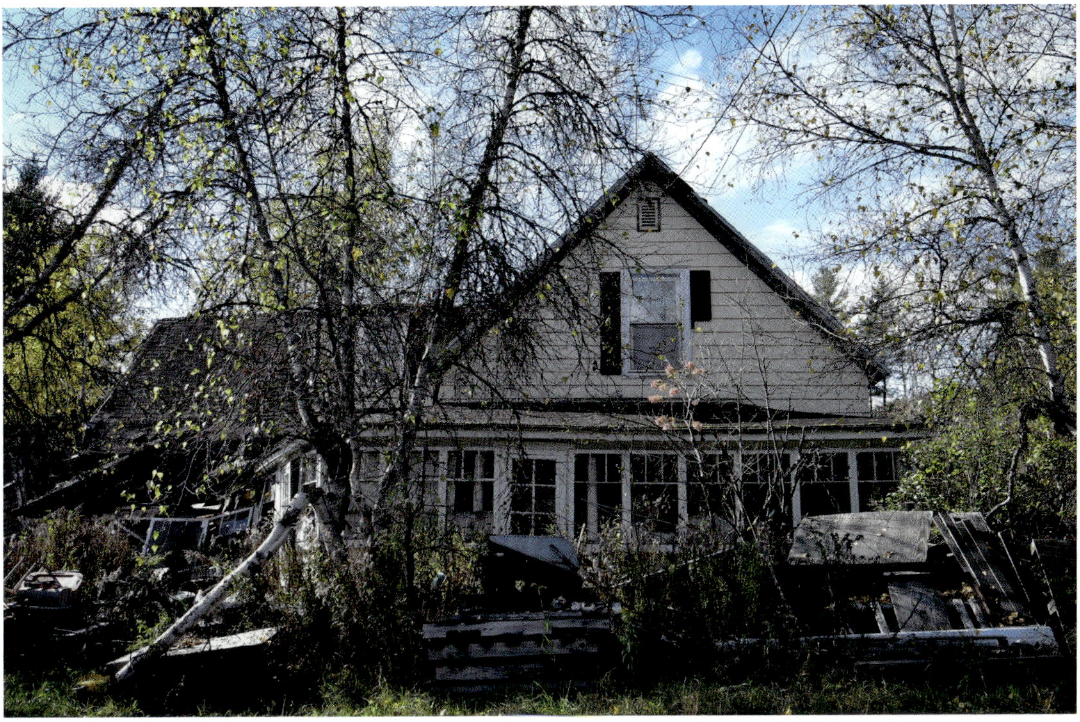

Above: So much gets left behind sometimes.

Right: A height chart I found scratched into an old door.

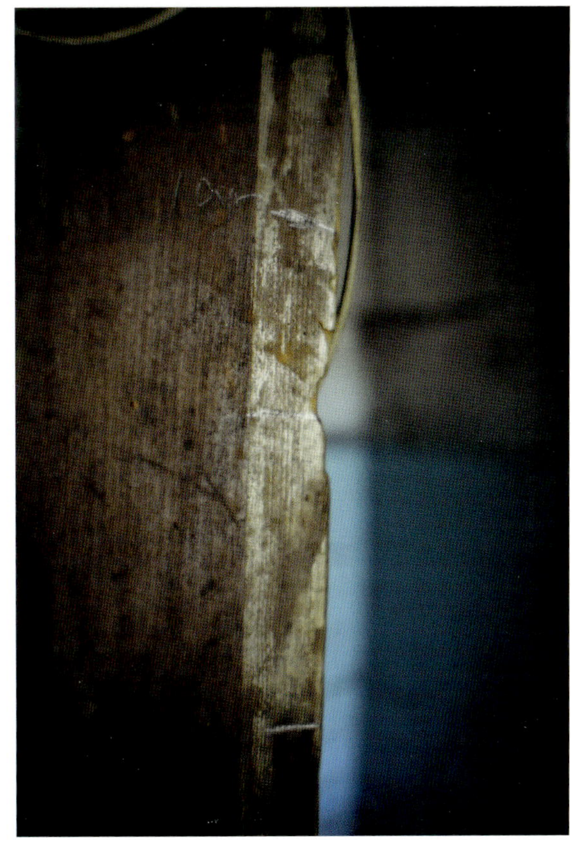

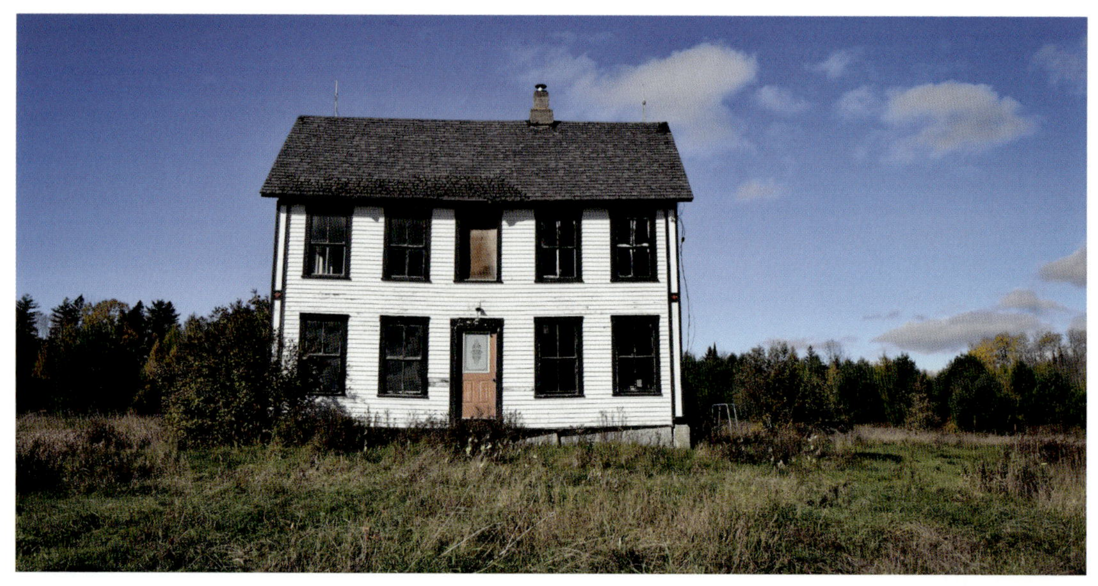

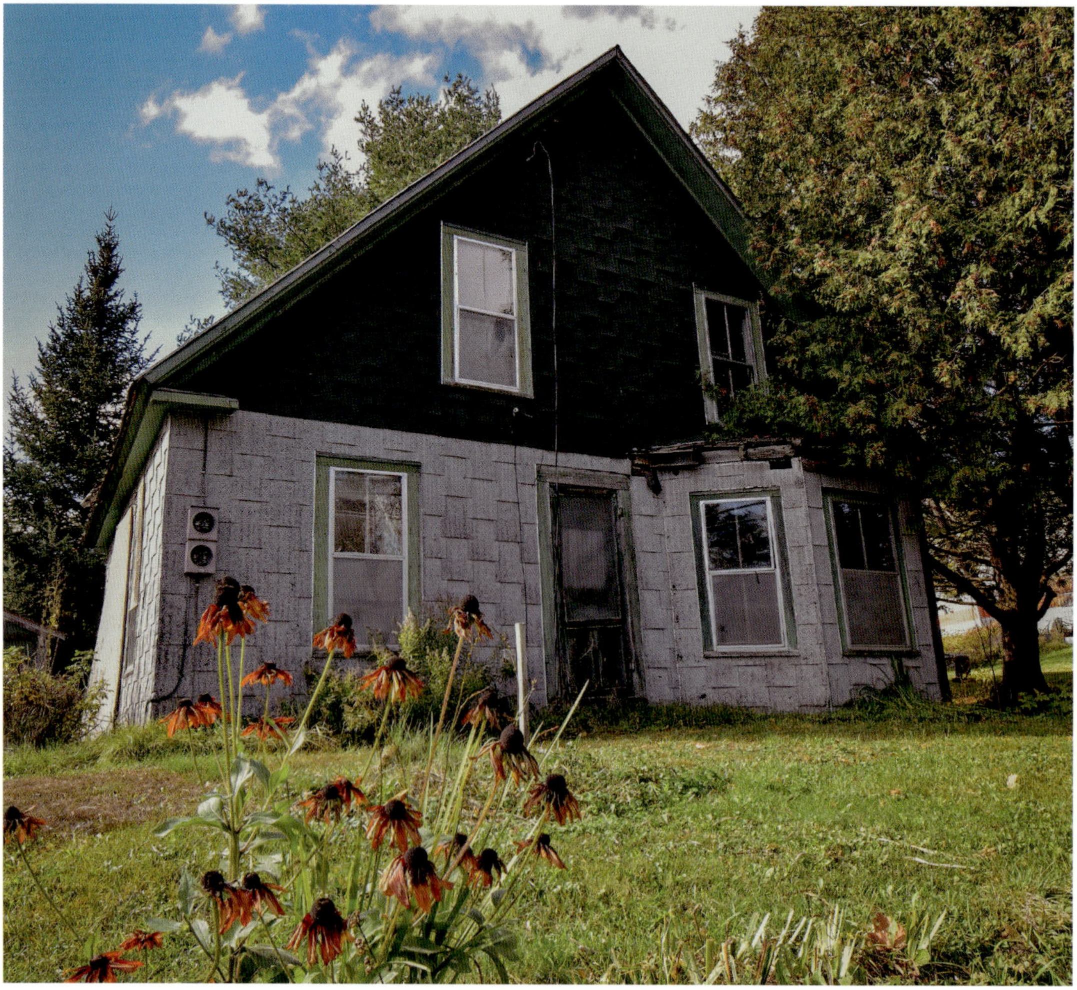

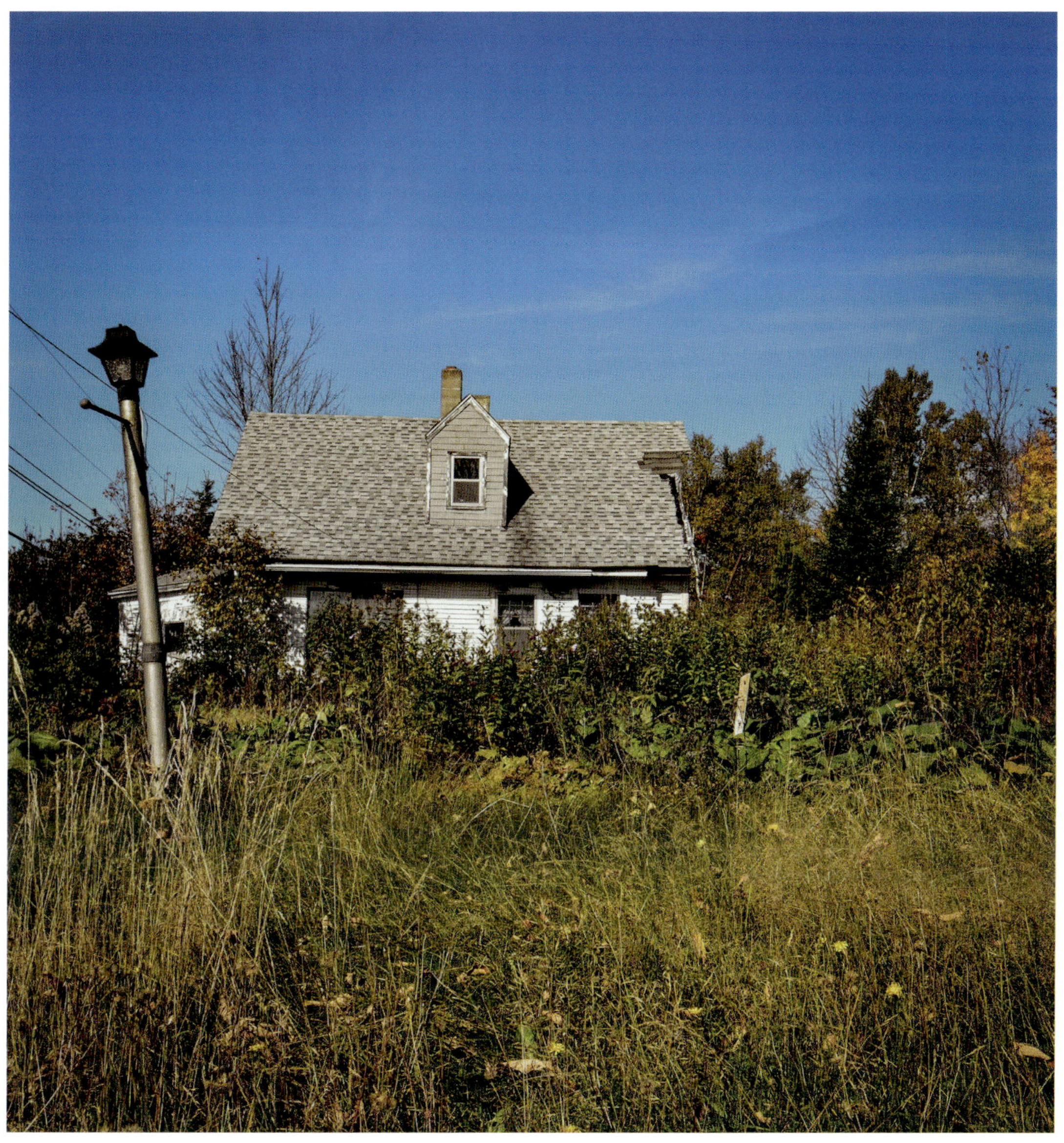

This lamppost hasn't welcomed anyone home in years. This house is all that is left standing of Puffert's and Gibson's Guest House and Cabins that started welcoming guests in the 1950s.

Opposite above: This house in northern Vermont stands in a large field with a rusty swing set to remind it of better days.

Opposite below: Boarded-up windows and no electricity.

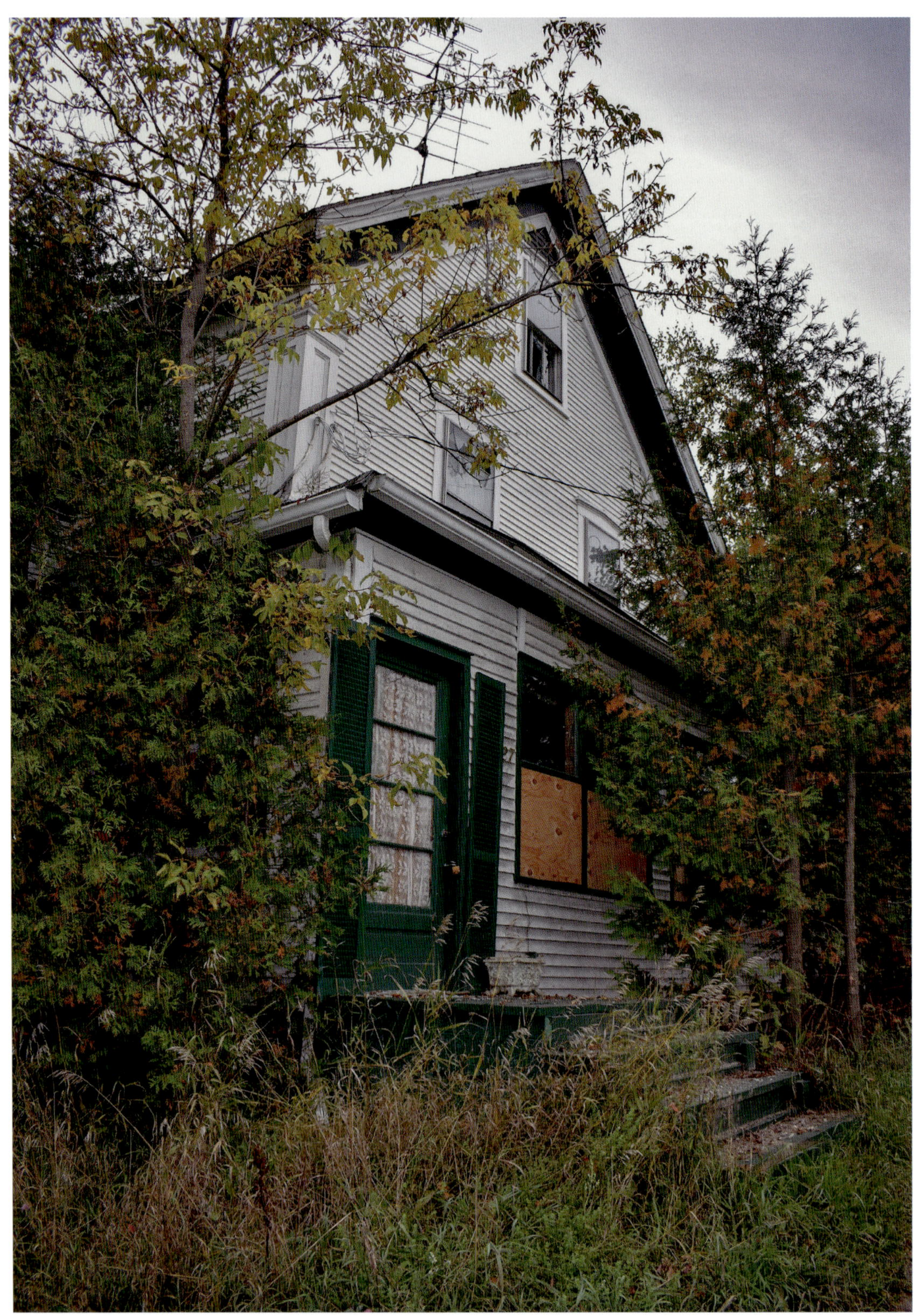

Right near the Canadian border, this house stands behind a wall of growth.

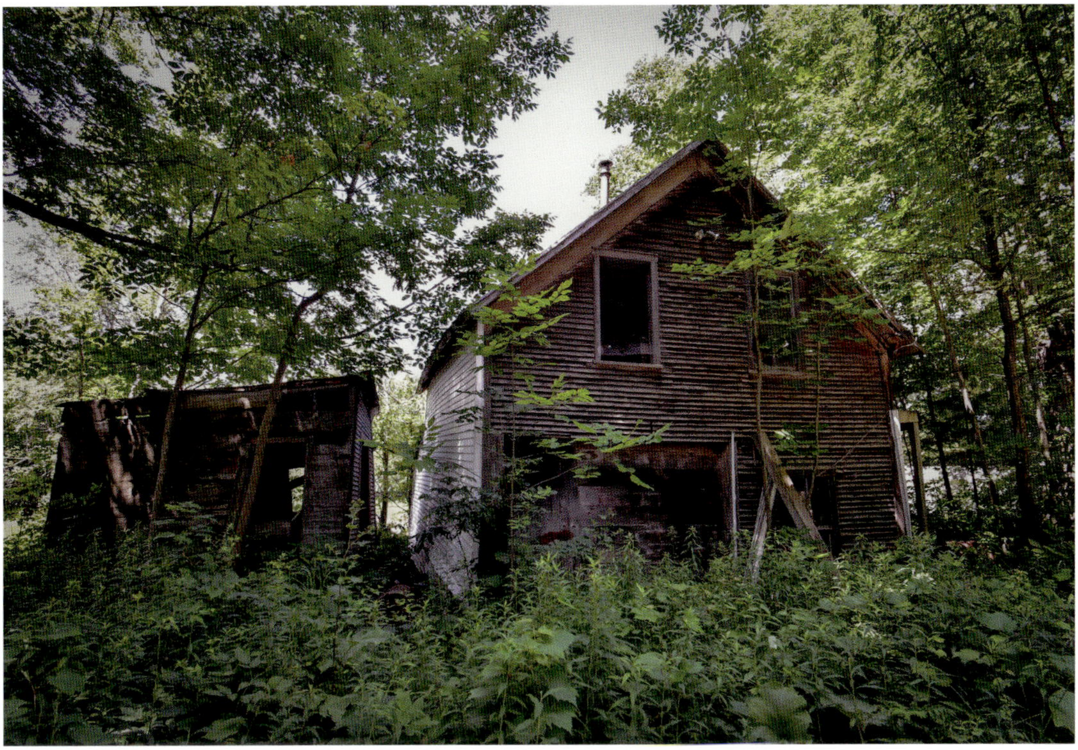

Former blacksmith shop.

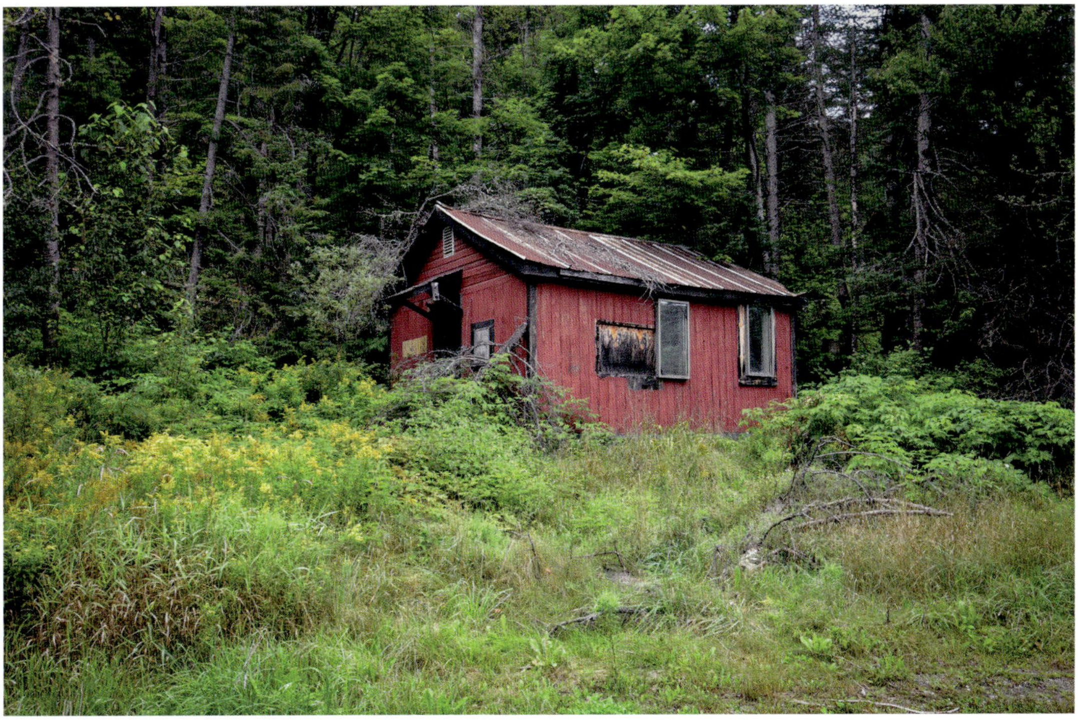

Another small, abandoned camp in northern New Hampshire.

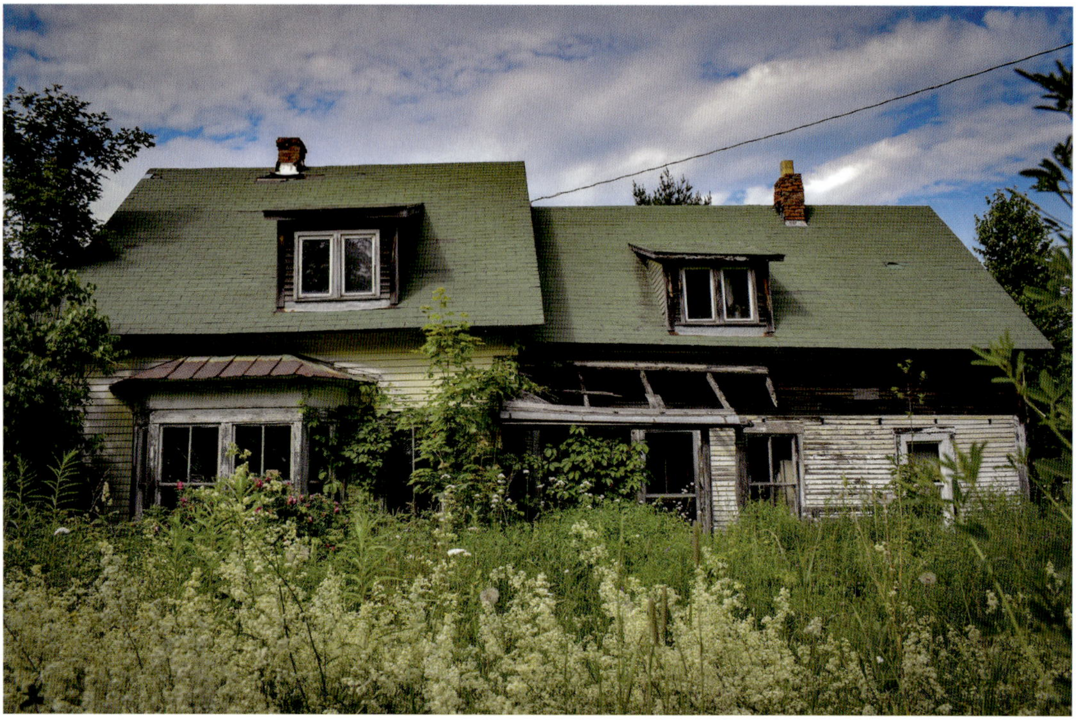

For a long time, local Vermonters spoke of this house sitting empty, but with a lone light bulb lighting the kitchen. That light has long since gone out.

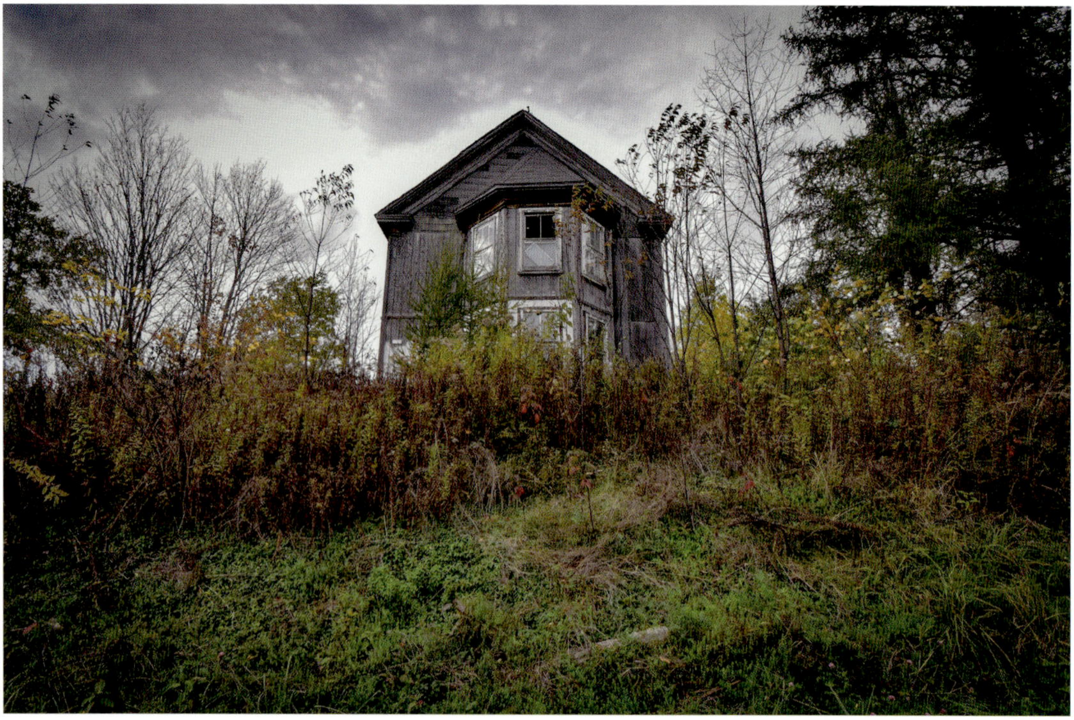

This old farmhouse in Vermont stands tall on an old highway, with a rusty farm truck in the driveway.

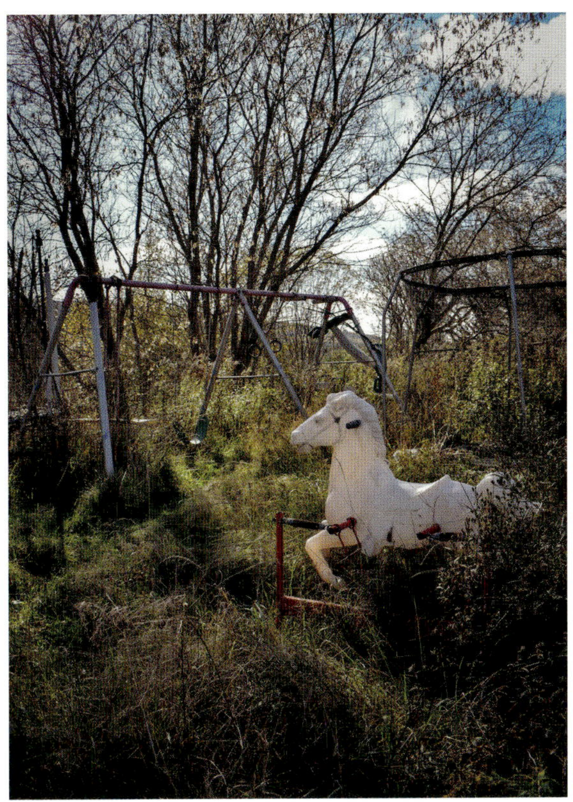

Right: The lonely, left-behind bouncy horse caught my eye at this abandoned house.

Below: Abandoned in a small, northern Vermont town.

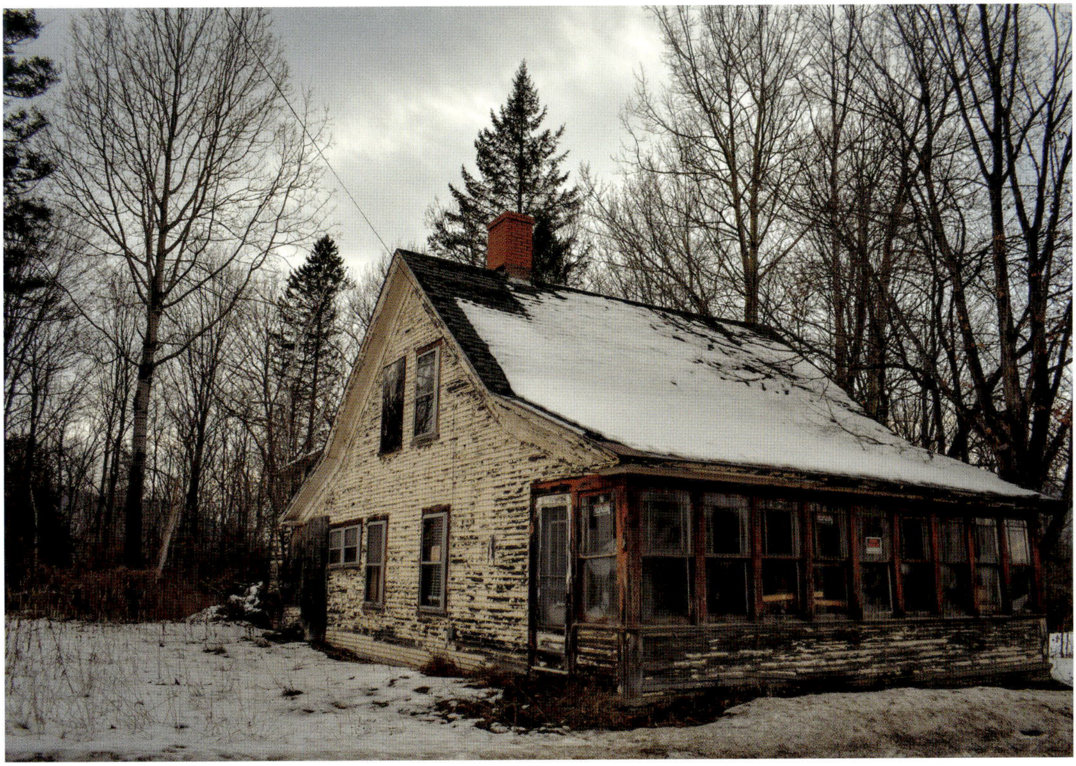

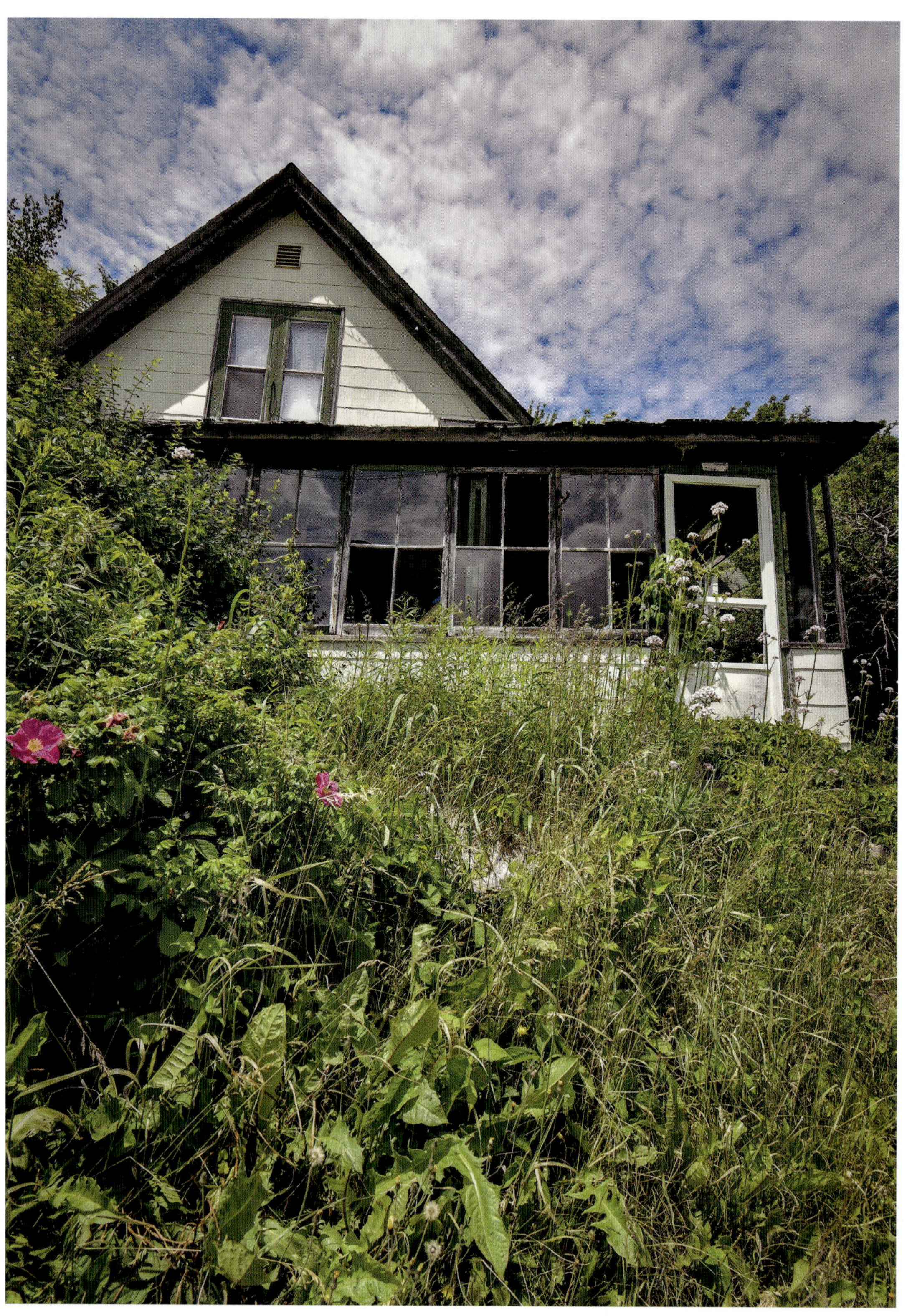

This house, near a stretch of abandoned tourist cabins, has also been left to fall apart.

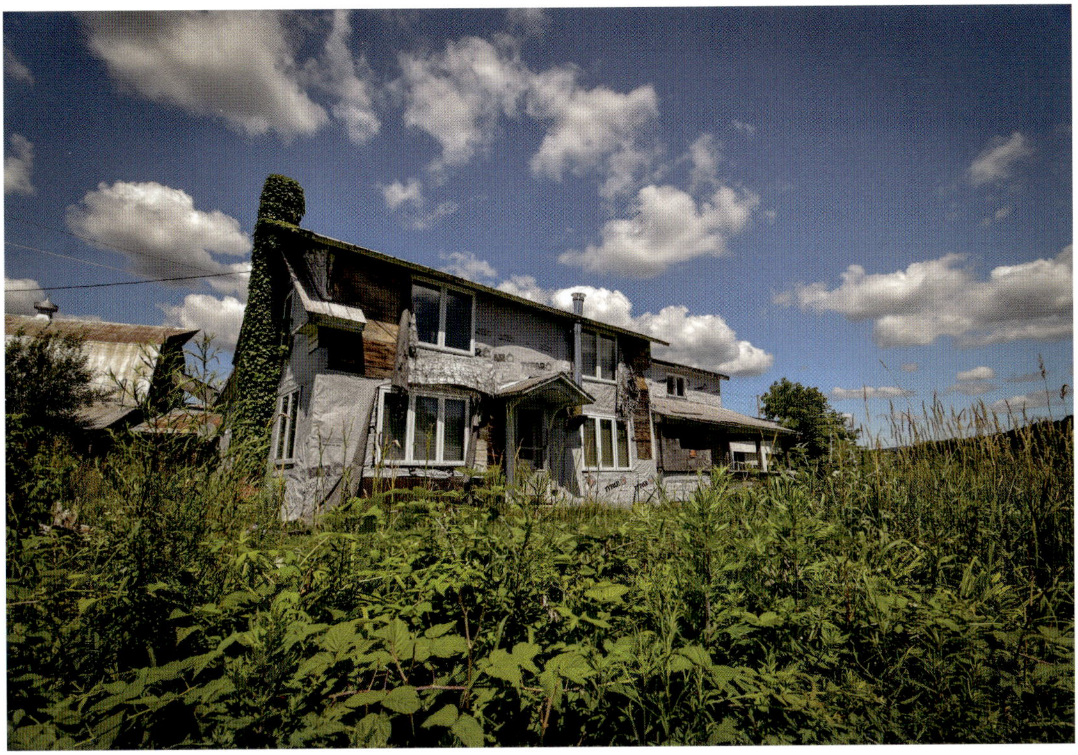

Above: Over a small bridge, this house sits unfinished and abandoned.

Right: A lonely chair outside of an abandoned cabin.

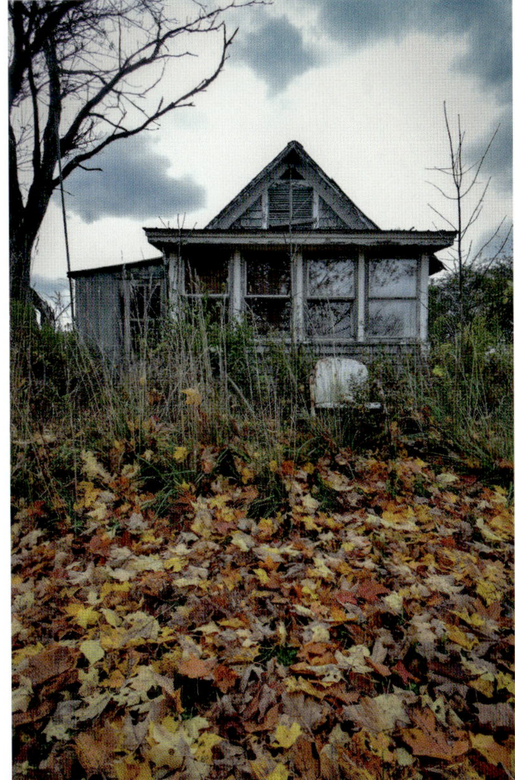

There are some houses that stick with you. It may be the timing of when you come across them, when you're feeling an extra sense of nostalgia or melancholy, or even some apprehensiveness. Those kinds of explores tend to be memorable. The day I found this house, it was a cool, dreary early October morning. The leaves had already started turning and falling and the dew was still saturating the ground, giving everything a little bit of a glistening effect. And then I saw it, this massive, dark house looming on top of a hill. It was hard to see at first because of the still-thick foliage that had yet to die off. I knew that the only way to get a closer look would be to climb up the hill, so I did my very best at bushwhacking my way through the overgrowth, over the musky-sweet smell of decaying leaves, armed with a stick in one hand and my camera around my neck. After my pants had caught on what seemed like every thorn on this crooked path I was attempting to create, I noticed that my sense of unease wasn't lessening, and I don't think it was just the sharp sting in my legs. I also began spotting large pieces of wood and window glass scattered around. Being sure to watch my footing, I decided to stop and take a few photos. Once I stopped walking, I finally realized just how quiet and still the area was. That's also when I picked up very clearly on my feeling of foreboding and I started wondering if maybe I wasn't alone. I decided that the photos I took were going to have to be good enough, and I turned to leave. As I did so, I heard leaves crunching in the not-so-far distance, and saw a truck slowly drive by at the bottom of the hill. Later, when speaking with my friend, Sonja, who had also been by this house in the past, she also said she felt a sense of unease, but also a sense of loneliness after seeing signs of a once busy homestead scattered around.

Most of the time, we never get to learn the stories of why places become, and often remain, abandoned and forgotten about. There are instances where houses become victims of our tragedies or the changes in our lives, just collateral damage of the human condition. They get discarded and left behind and have a history forced upon them that they are then left with, while people can often move on and leave it all behind if they choose to. Houses, like people, often get defined by the stories and tragedies they have no real control over.

Sometimes houses, through no fault of their own, end up abandoned and forgotten—even the ones that were once loved by many. One house, with its beautiful Greek-Revival accents, has sat abandoned for years in northern New Hampshire. Last lived in around the early 2000s and purchased but then left to decay for the past several years, the north country has started truly wearing on the gorgeous woodwork of this now neglected farmhouse. In speaking with a niece of the Cotter family, who were the original owners of the house, I learned that it was once a home full of love and well-kept memories. The family immigrated to the United States from Canada and chose to raise their fourteen children on this rural farmstead.

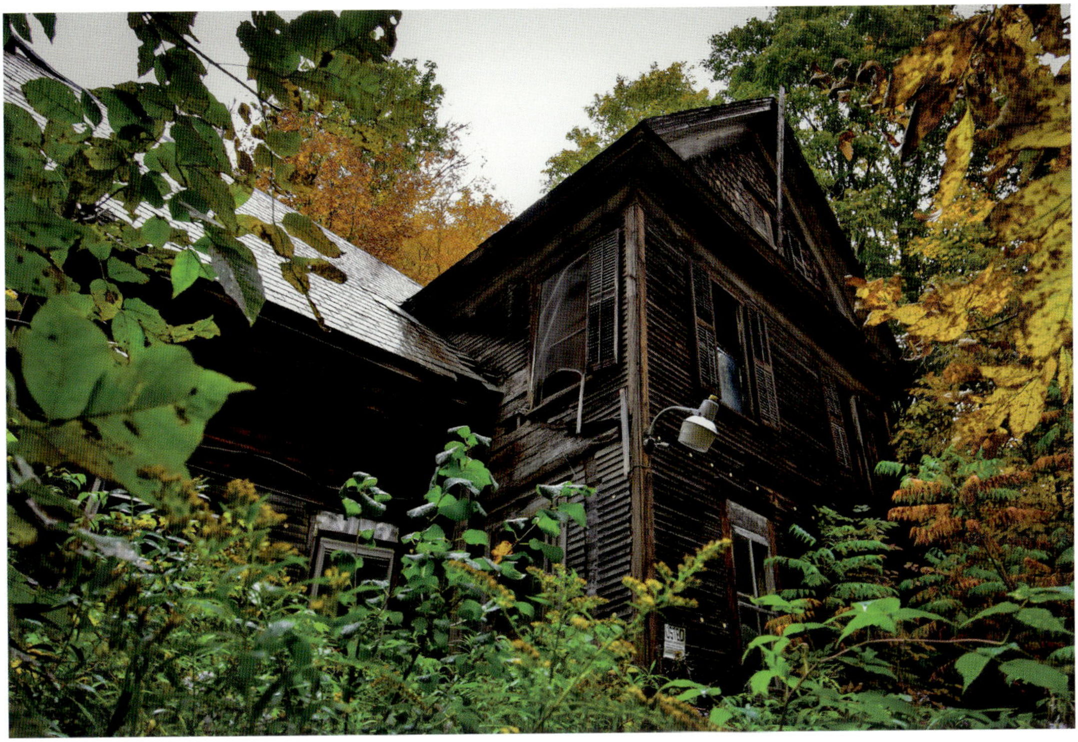

Decaying on the hill in Vermont.

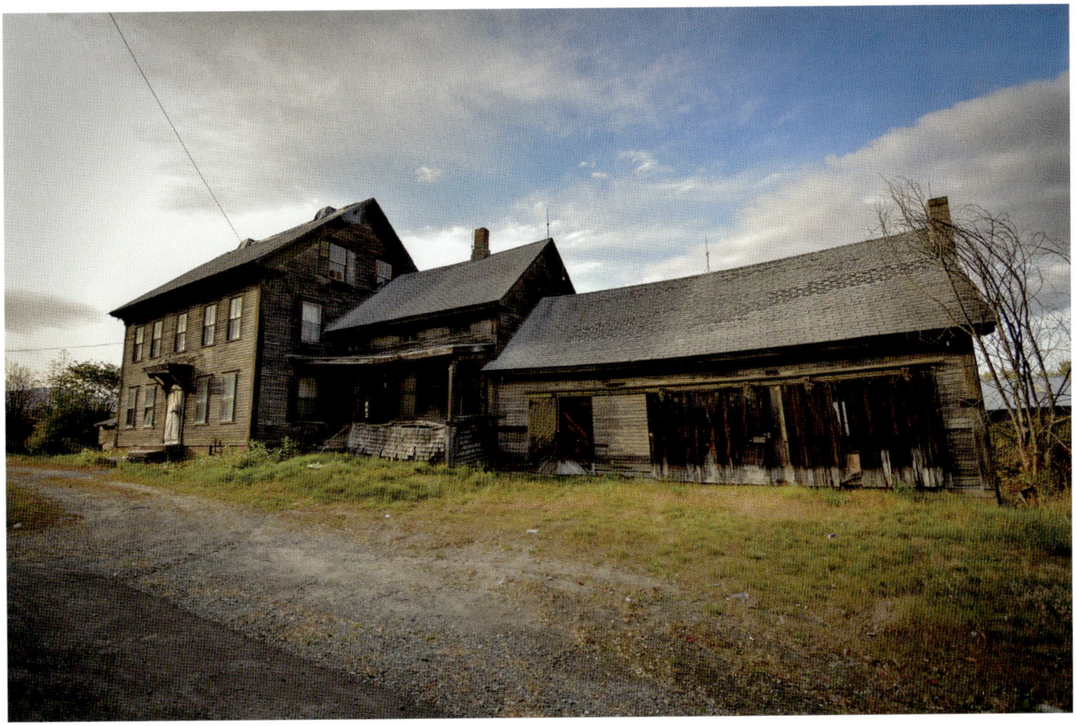

The once loved Cotter farmhouse with Greek-Revival architectural accents.

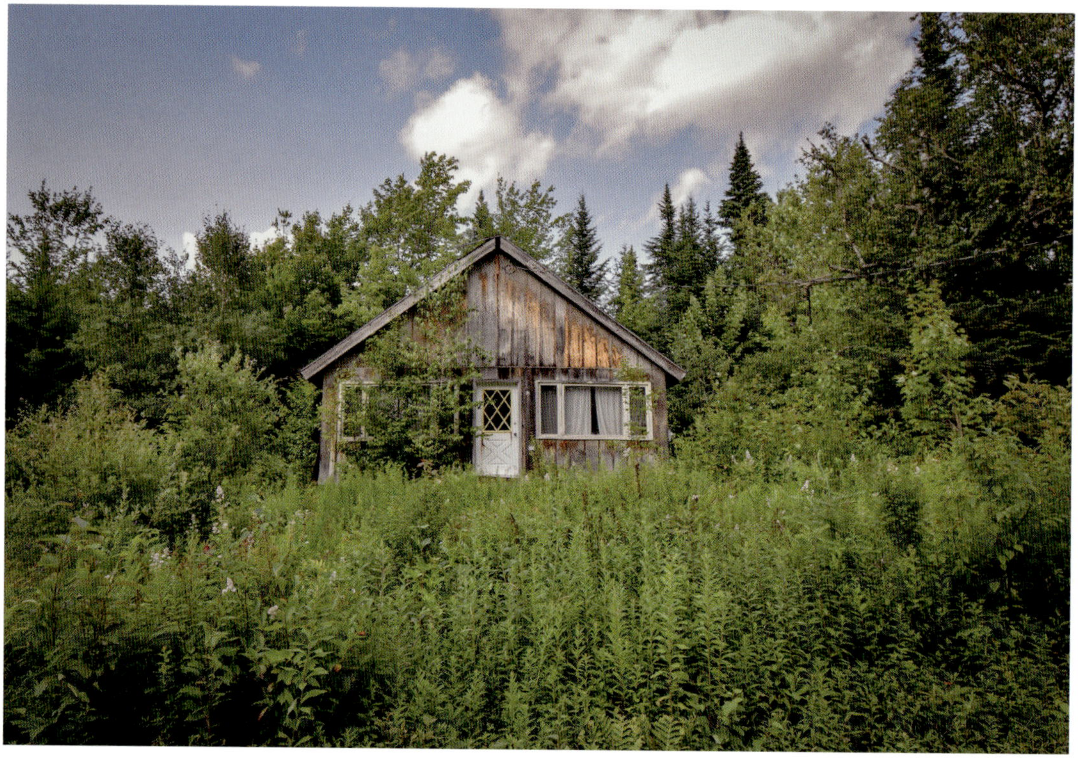

A once-loved cottage on the way to the lake.

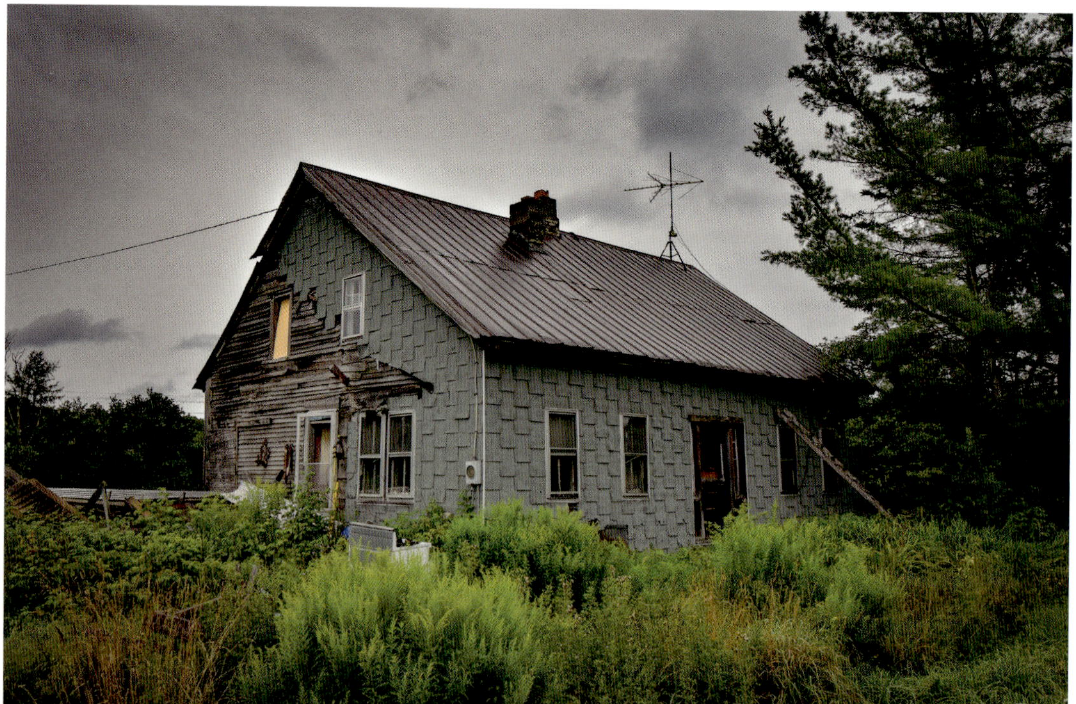

A ladder leans against the house, a reminder that this house was once cared for.

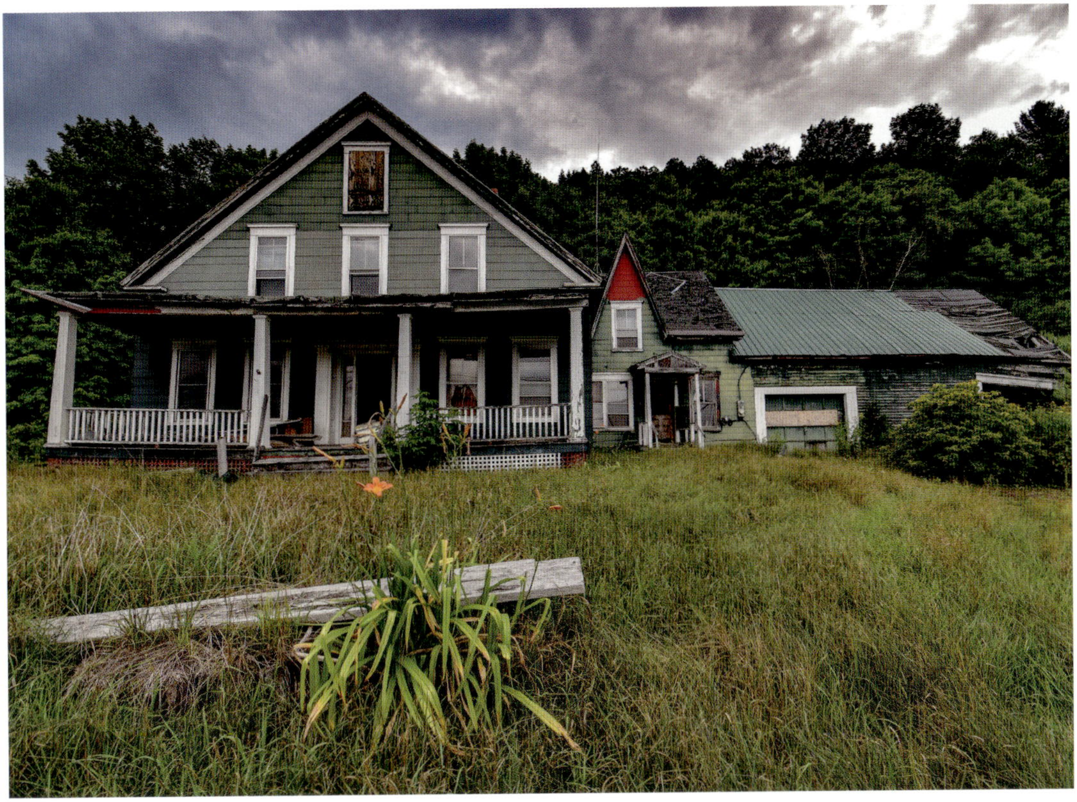

Above: I like to call this large, rambling house in northern New Hampshire the "patchwork house" because of the assorted colors of roofing and paint that somehow give it a slight whimsical appearance.

Right: A small camp in the woods of Vermont.

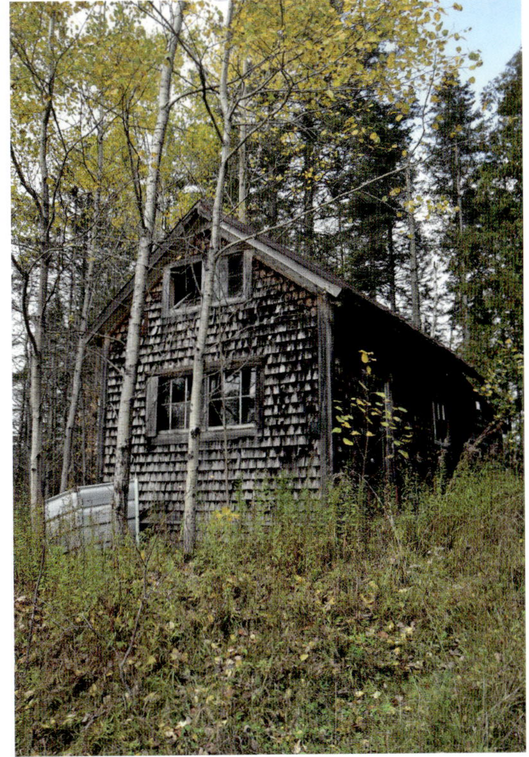

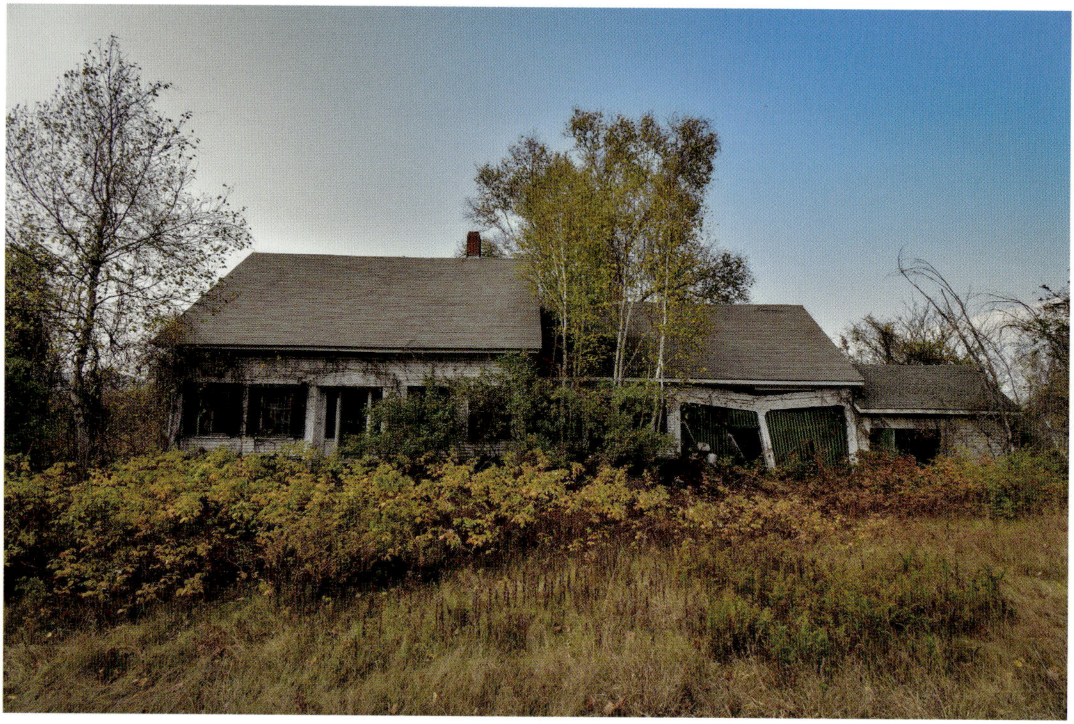

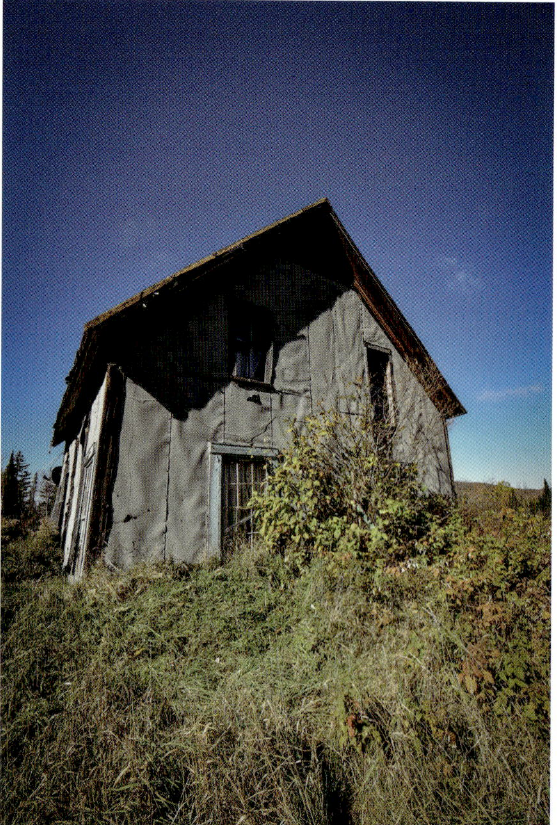

Above: Sitting close to the road, this house with its wall of uninviting overgrowth hides with rotting floors and decaying memories inside.

Left: An old farmhouse found off one of Vermont's many winding backroads.

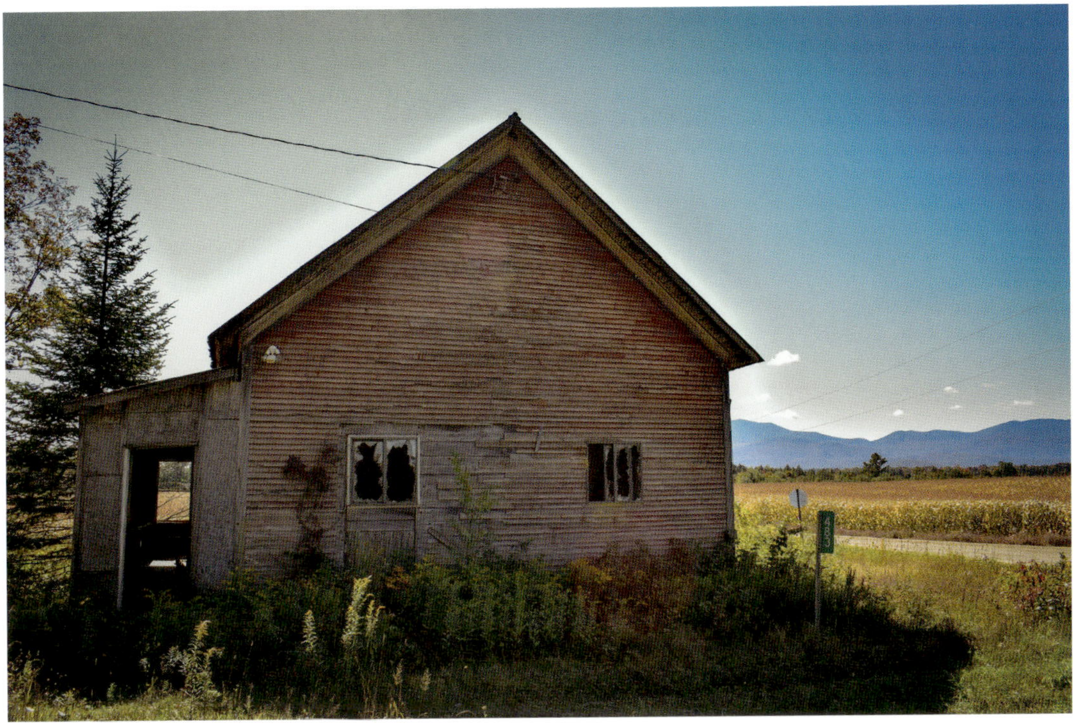

Above: In the 1960s, this building was used as a schoolhouse. It now sits empty across the road from a graveyard.

Right: Views of the graveyard across the road from the old schoolhouse.

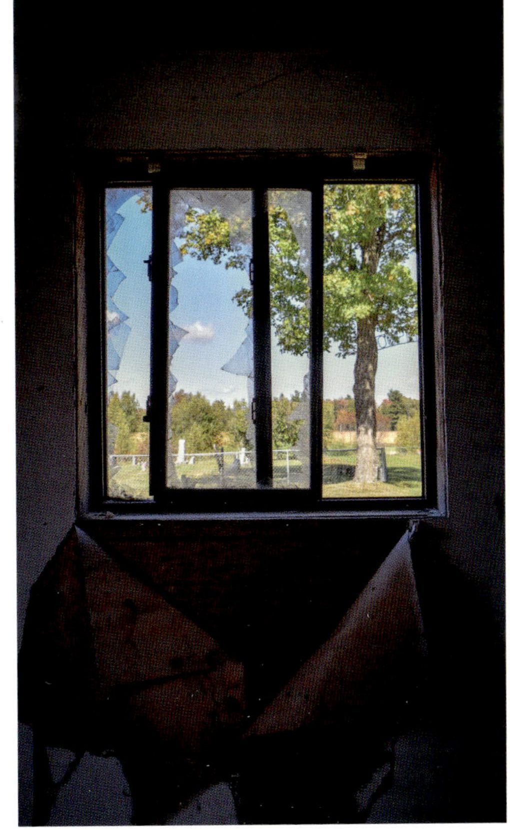

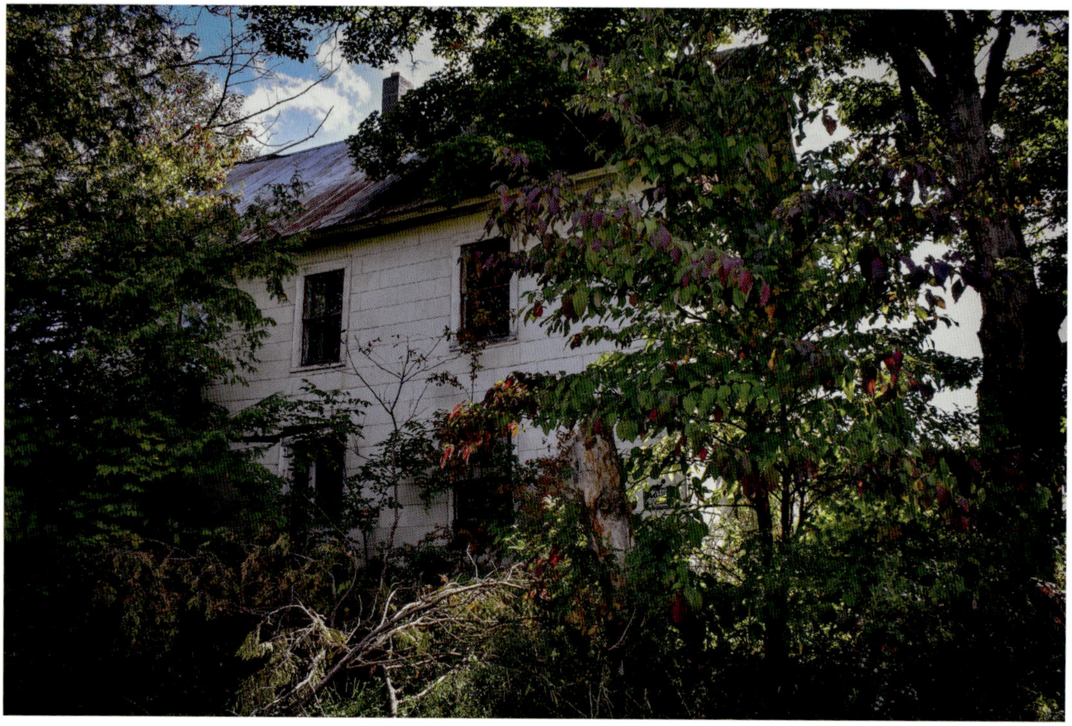

This house, though empty and forgotten, sits close to the town green, where local families still gather and create new memories.

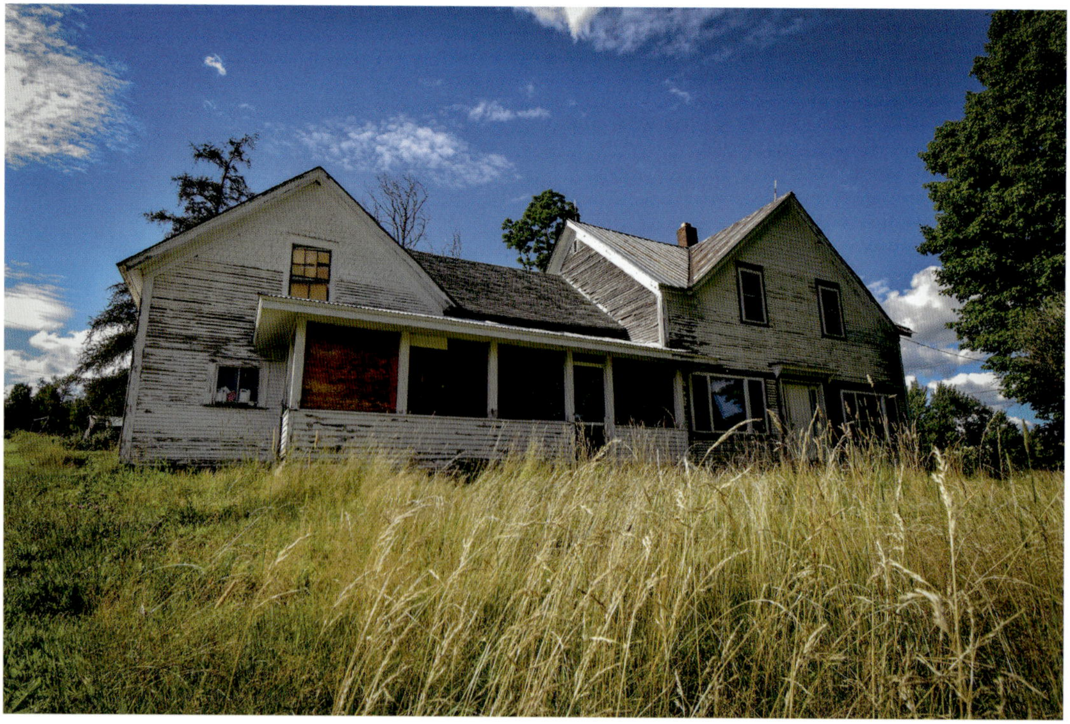

Blue skies and broken windows.

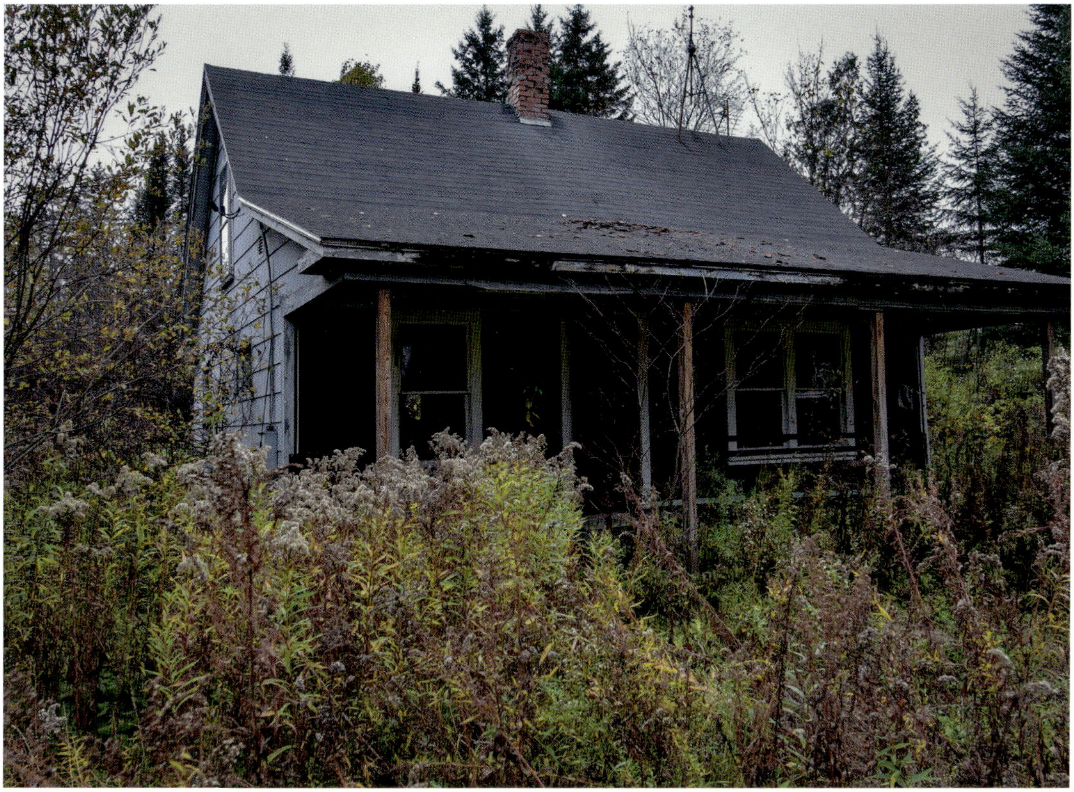

Above: Despite being abandoned, this house has held up well in the harsh Vermont winters.

Right: Not far from a busy tourist area, this windowless, doorless, and practically floorless house is falling apart.

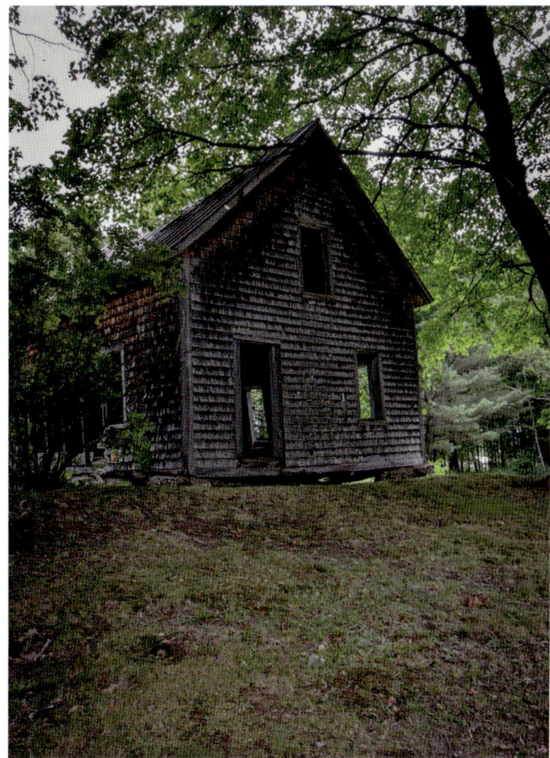

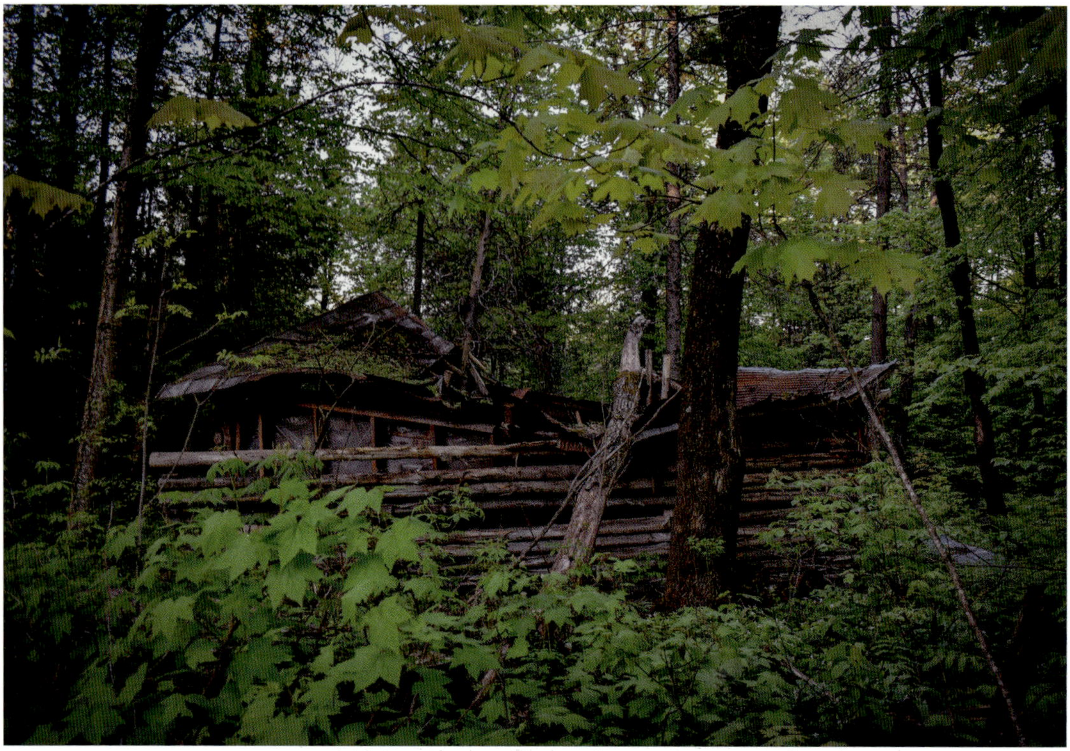

Almost completely gone.

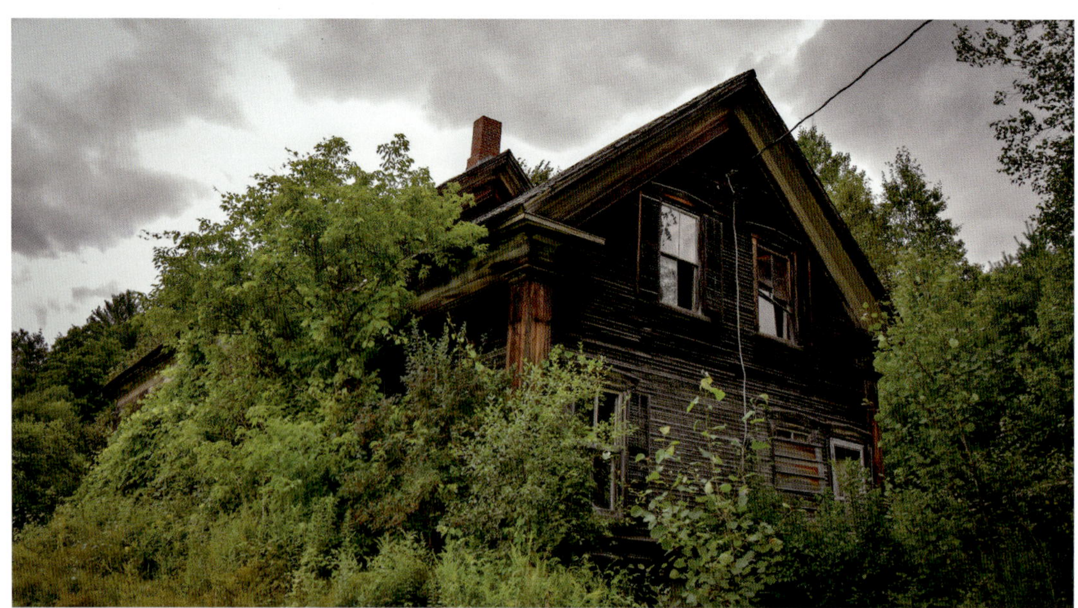

On a bend in the road stands a house that is covered in so much warm weather foliage, you may miss it if you blink. I've passed this house numerous times, during every season, and am always in awe of the beautiful architecture that has somehow withstood years of abandonment and neglect. Sometime before 2013, it appeared that someone had started working on restoring the house, though, as they sometimes do, those best laid plans may have fallen through, as it has sat untouched since.

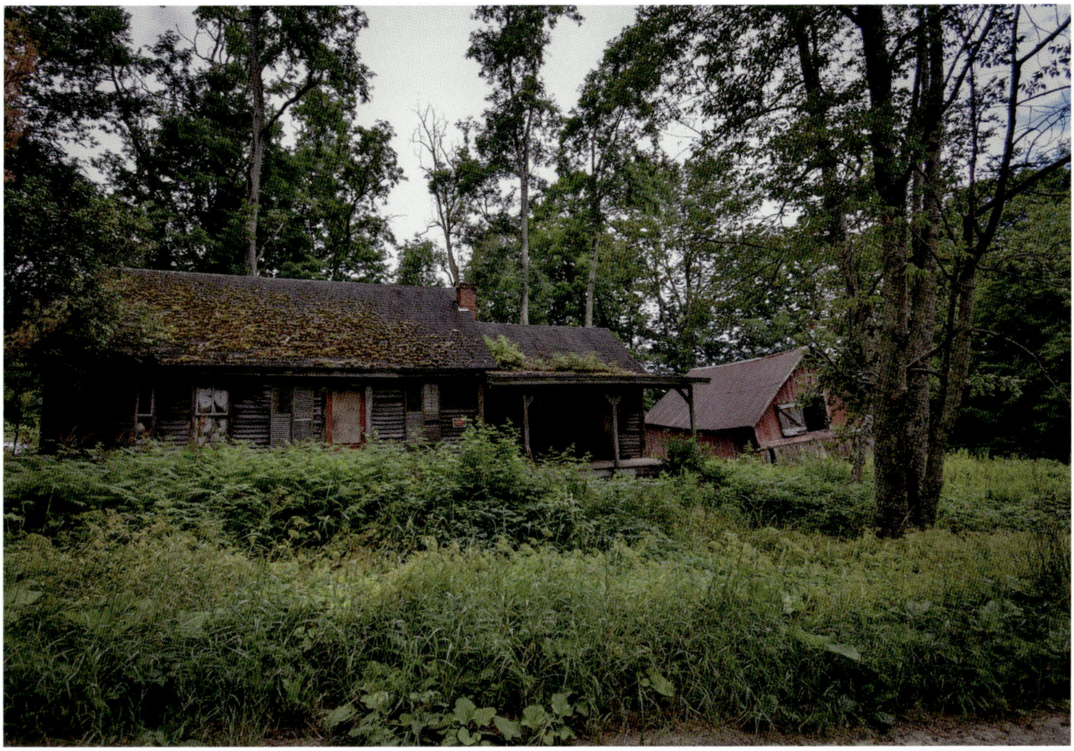

Mossy roof.

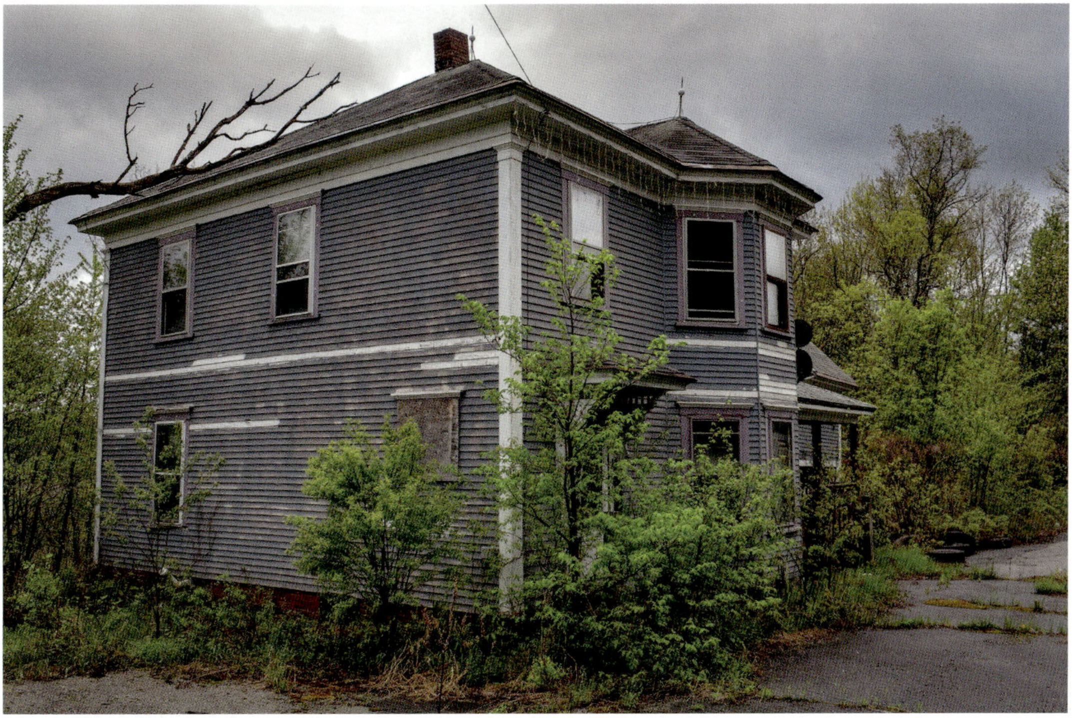

One of the first abandoned houses I came across in northeastern Vermont, also known as the "Northeast Kingdom."

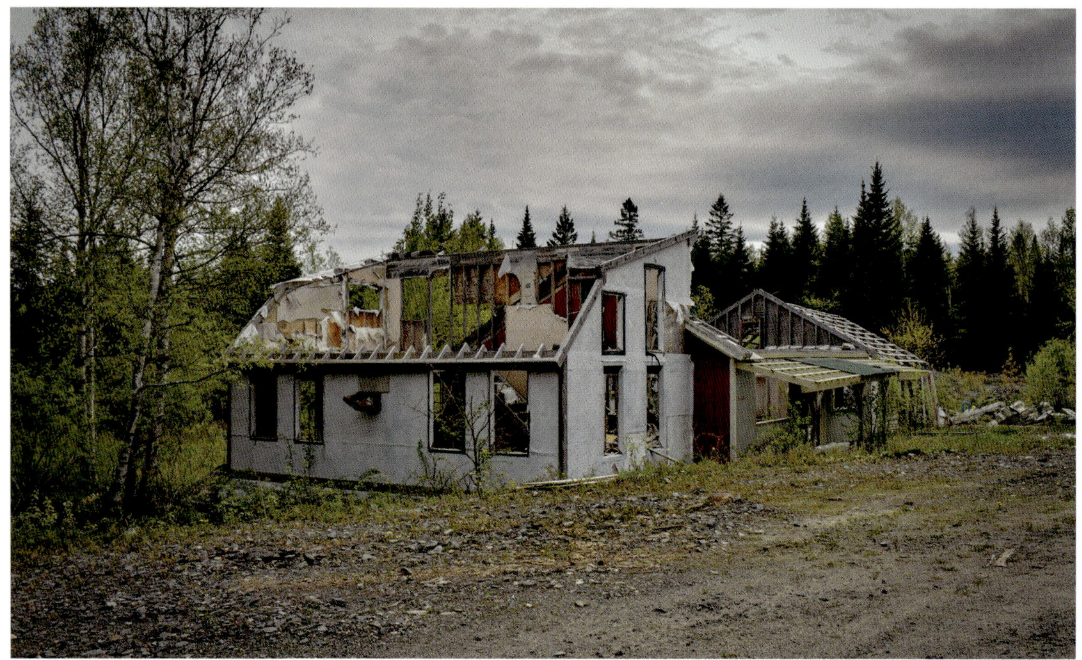

This house, or business, or whatever it may have been in its past life, was another that has stuck with me long after I found it. The road itself is twisty and desolate, connecting one small town to another. When I came around a corner, this wasn't what I was expecting to see. One side appears to have a more home-like feel to it, with remnants of a fireplace, while the other side could have potentially been a business of sorts.

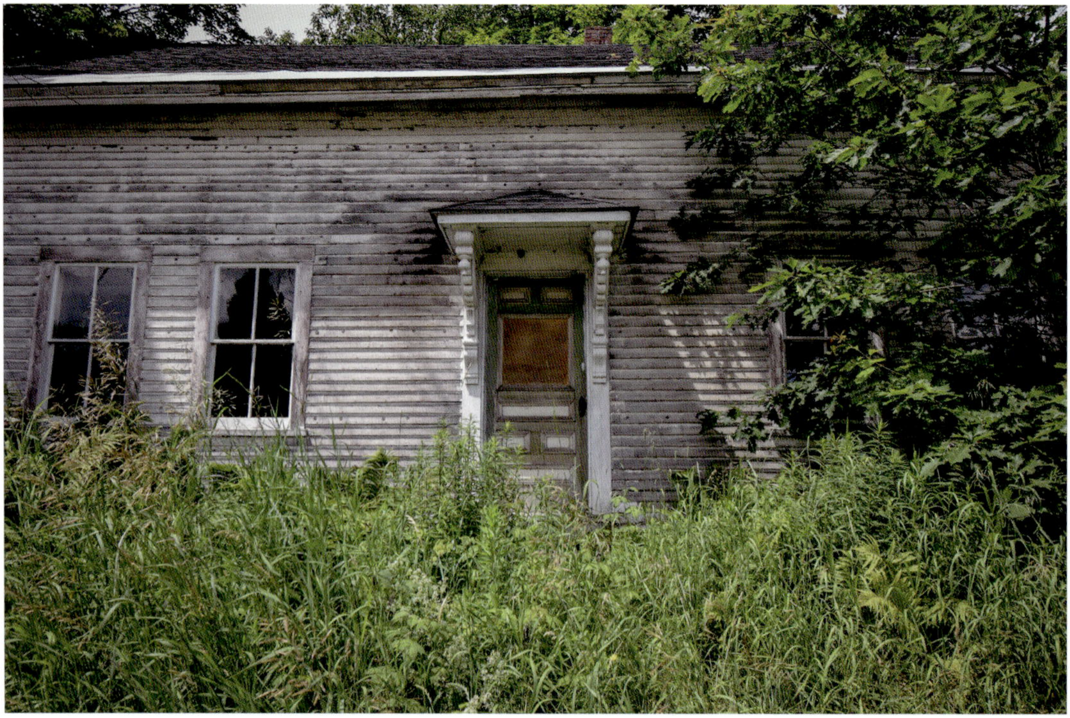

The craftsmanship of this doorway caught my eye in northern New Hampshire.

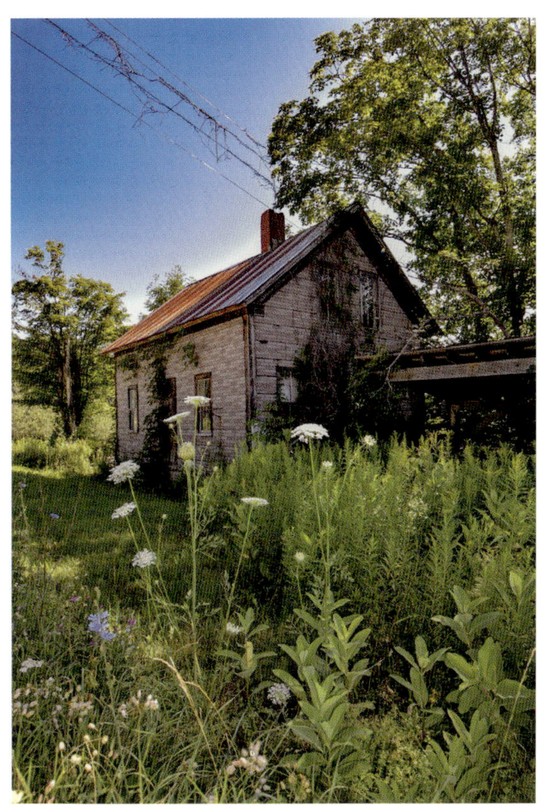

Right: Small, abandoned house among the flowers.

Below: An abandoned farmstead near a lake in northeastern Vermont.

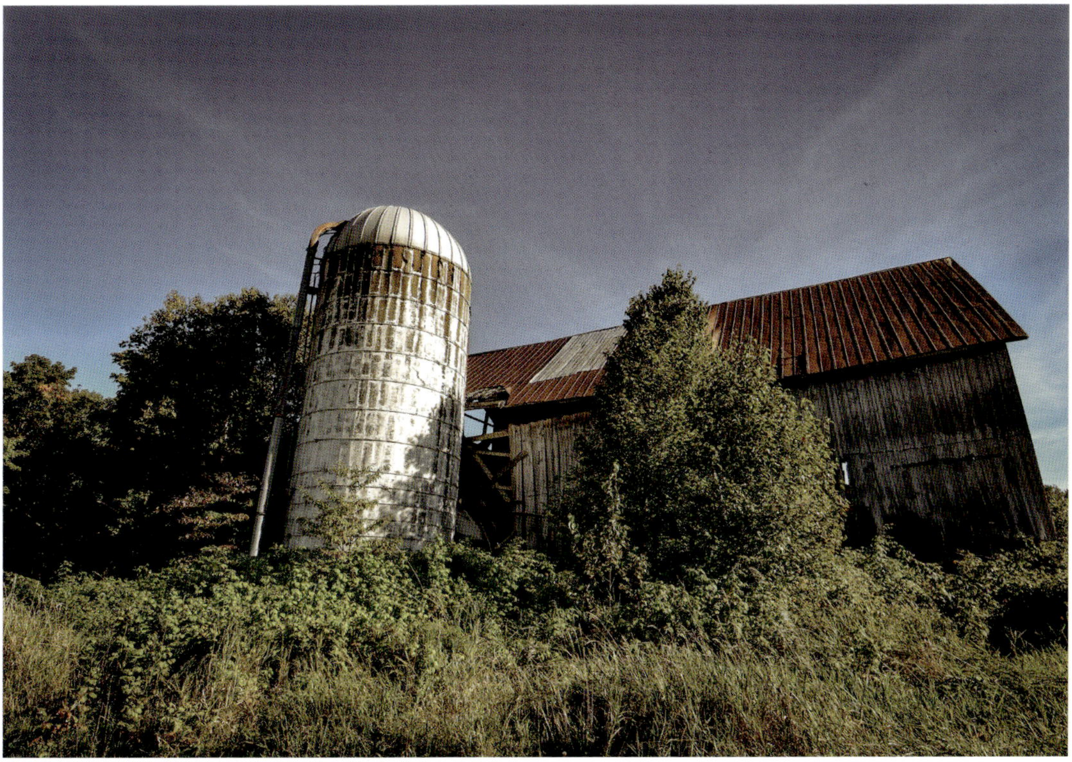

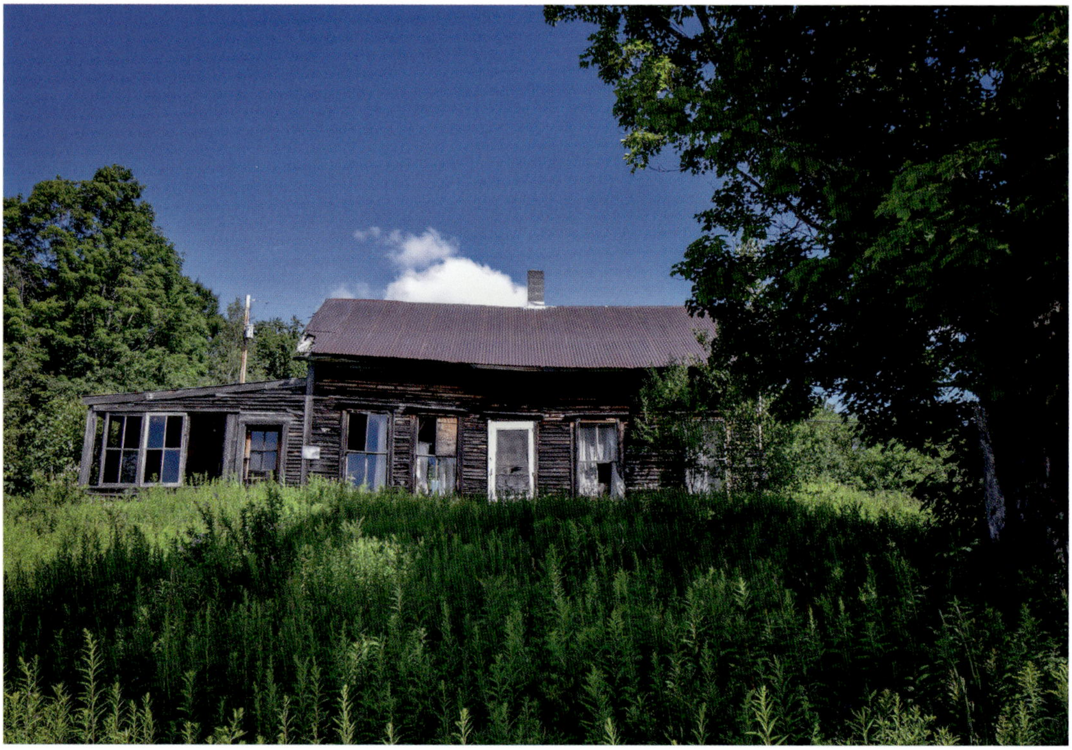

Broken windows and broken dreams.

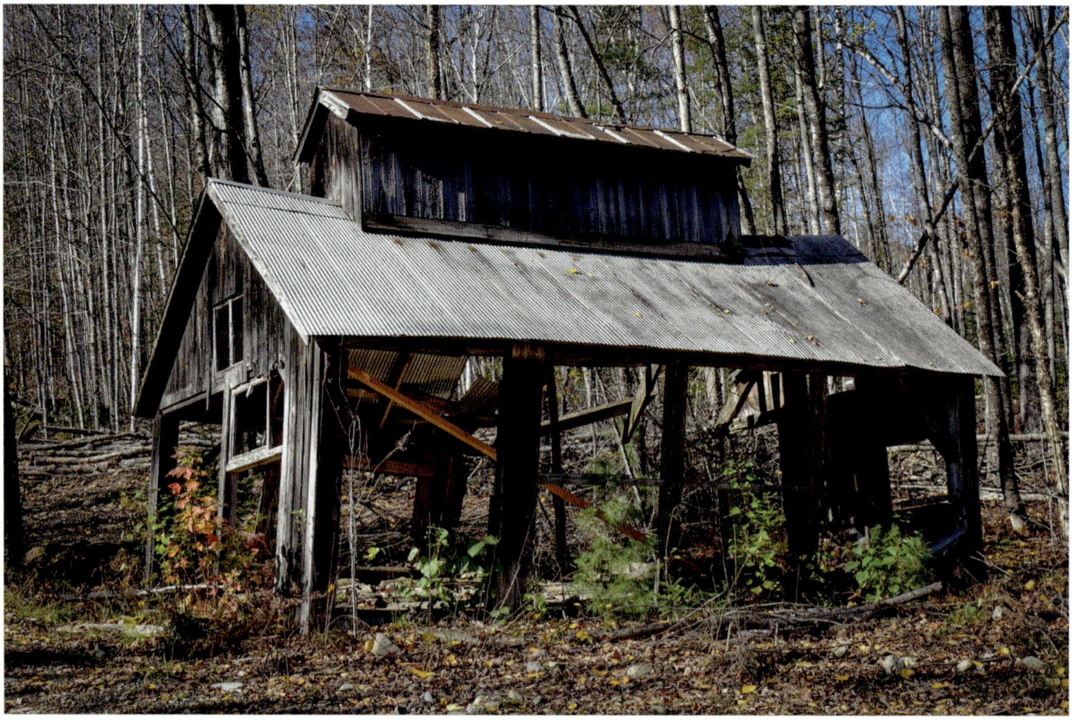

Dilapidated sugar shacks aren't uncommon around Vermont.

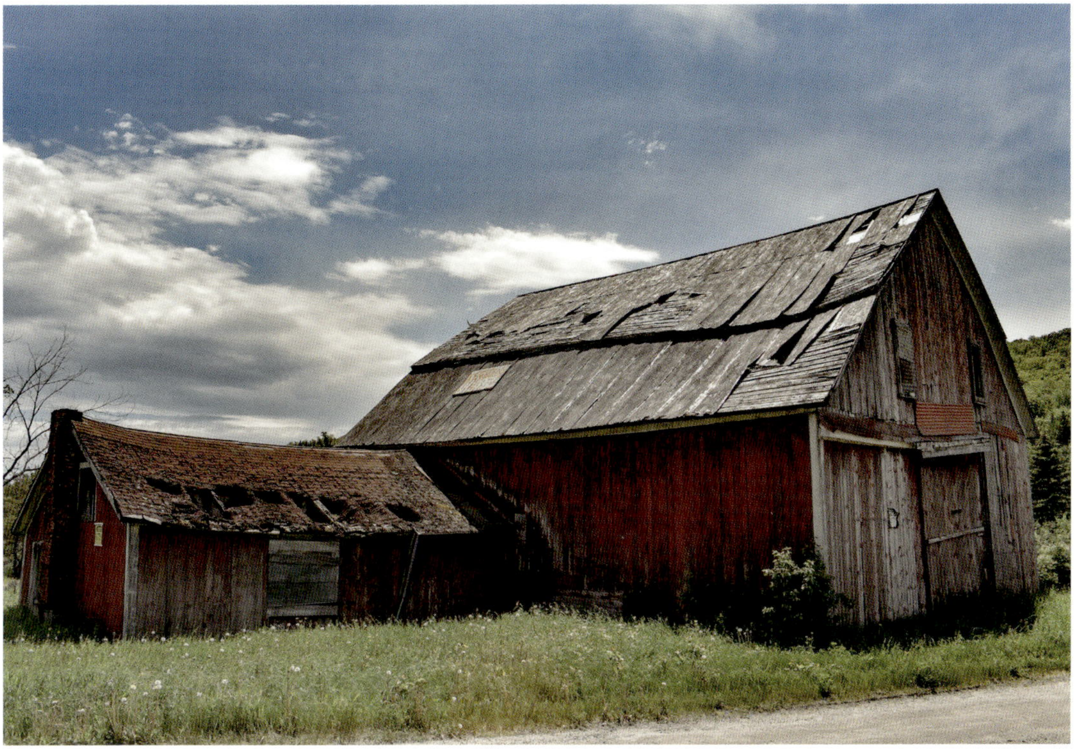

At one point, this structure was a small house with an attached barn.

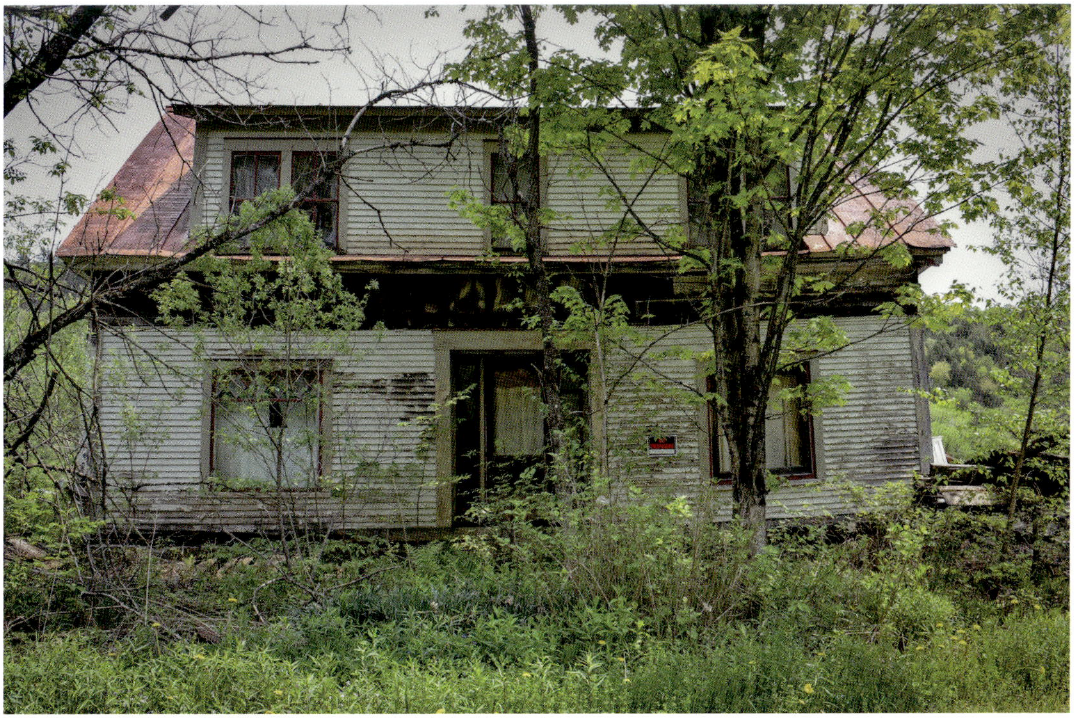

Abandoned on the side of the road.

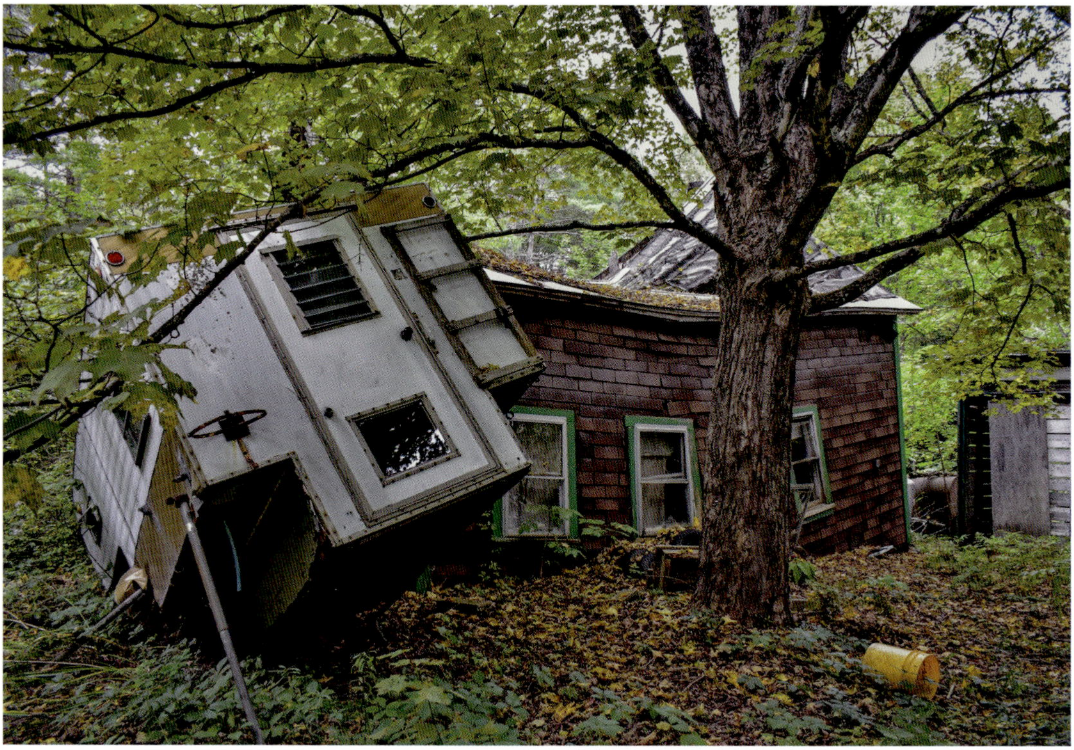

When two homes become abandoned.

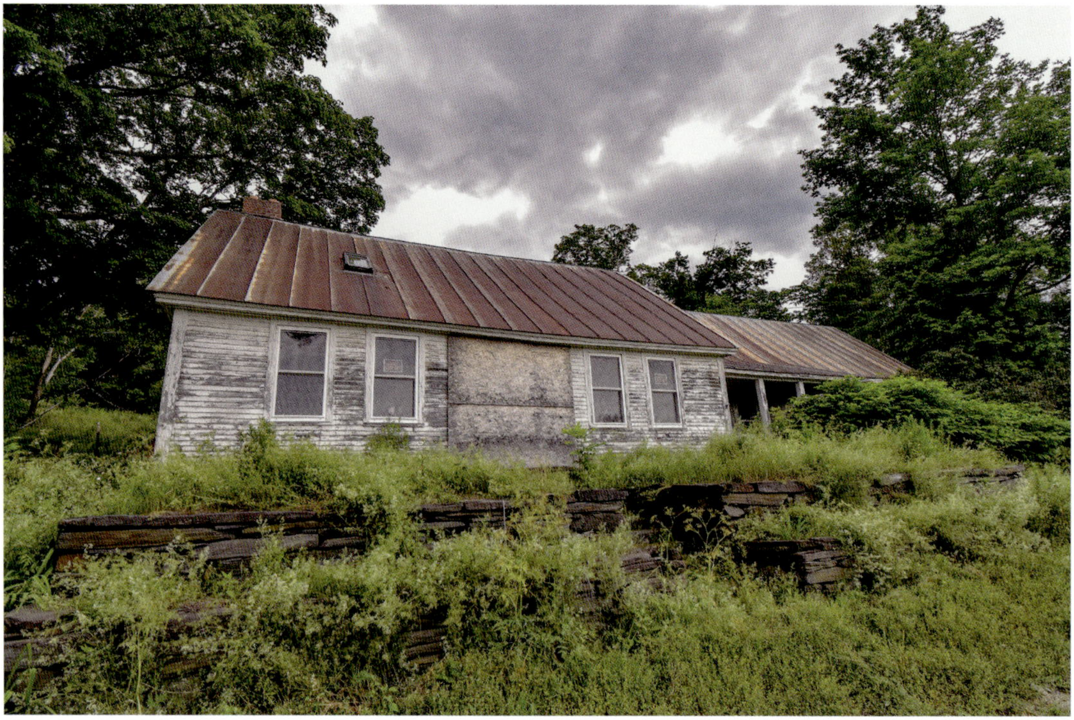

Abandoned farmhouse.

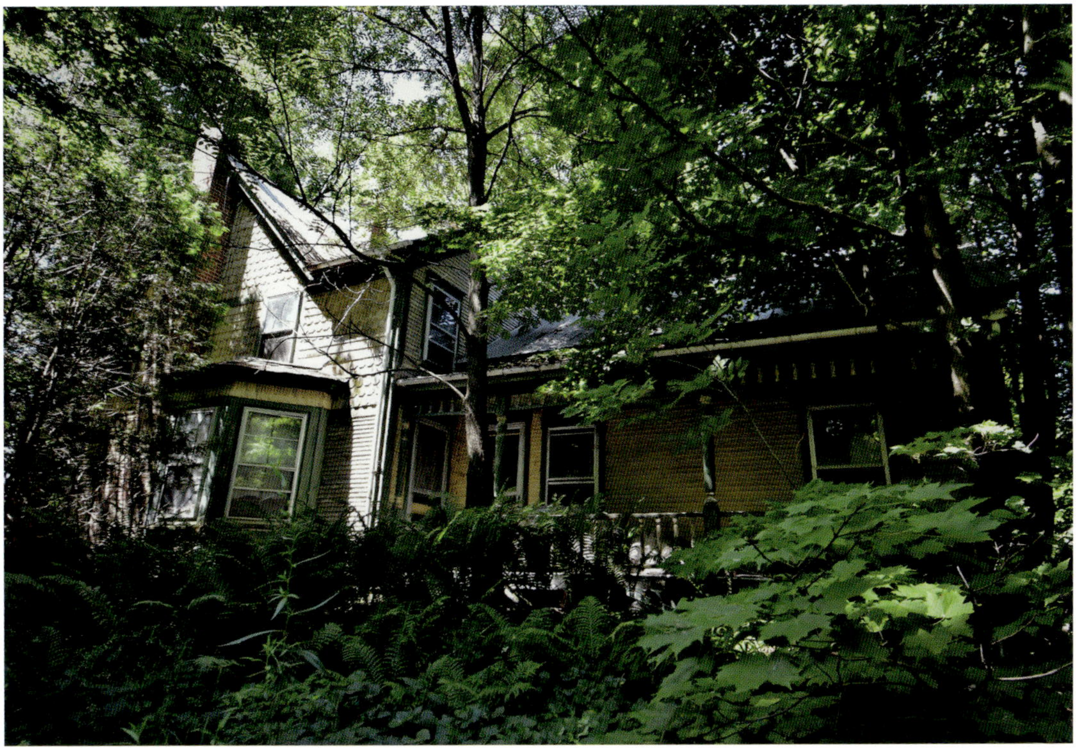

Another old farmhouse, with sunlight peeking through.

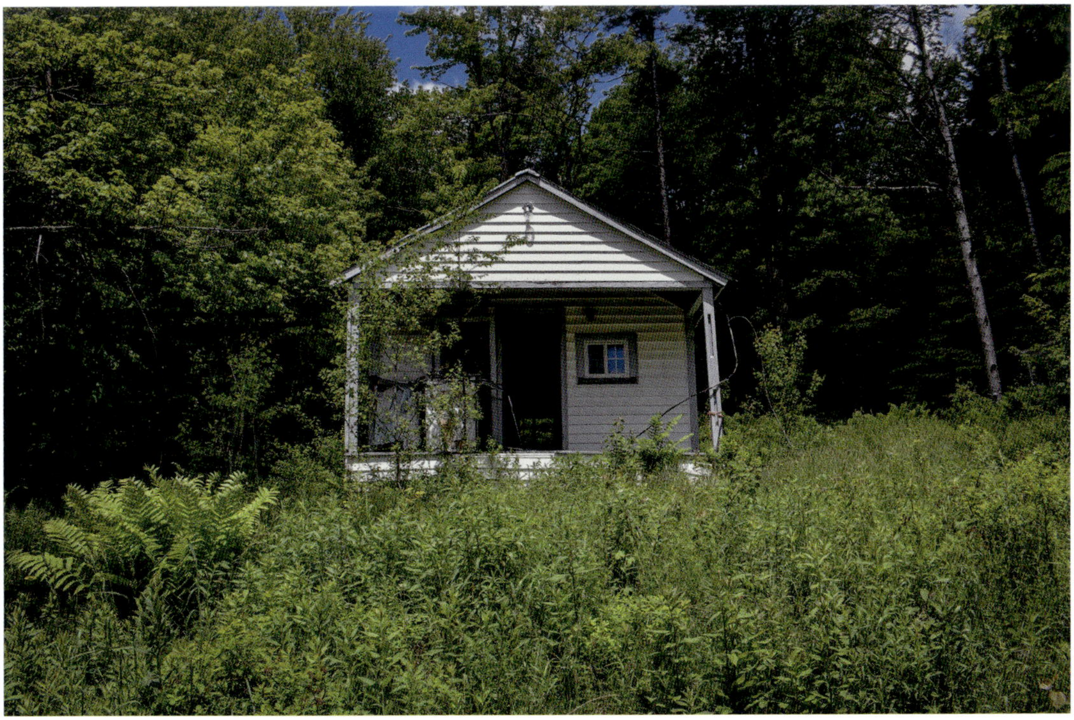

Another abandoned camp.

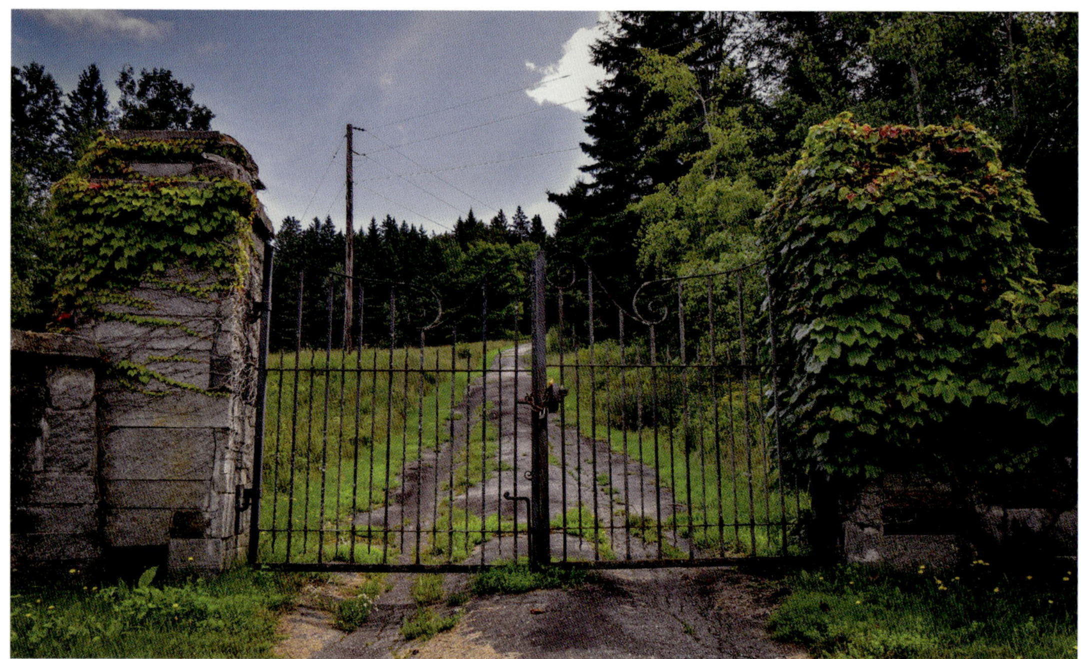

I have driven past this gate numerous times, and always wondered what was behind it, up the long driveway. The property was purchased by proponents of a project which was a controversial proposal to run over 190 miles of power lines from Canada to northern New Hampshire. The NH Supreme Court voted to uphold the rejection of the proposal. The log cabin that sits on the property has remained abandoned, locked behind the rusting gate.

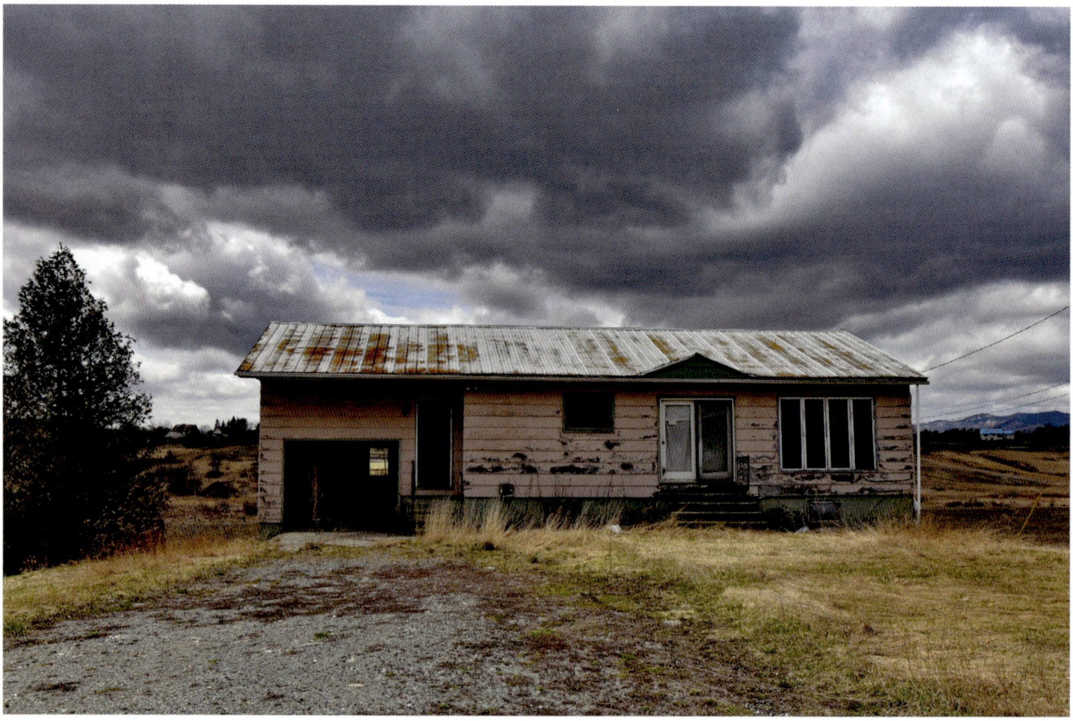

Little pink houses.

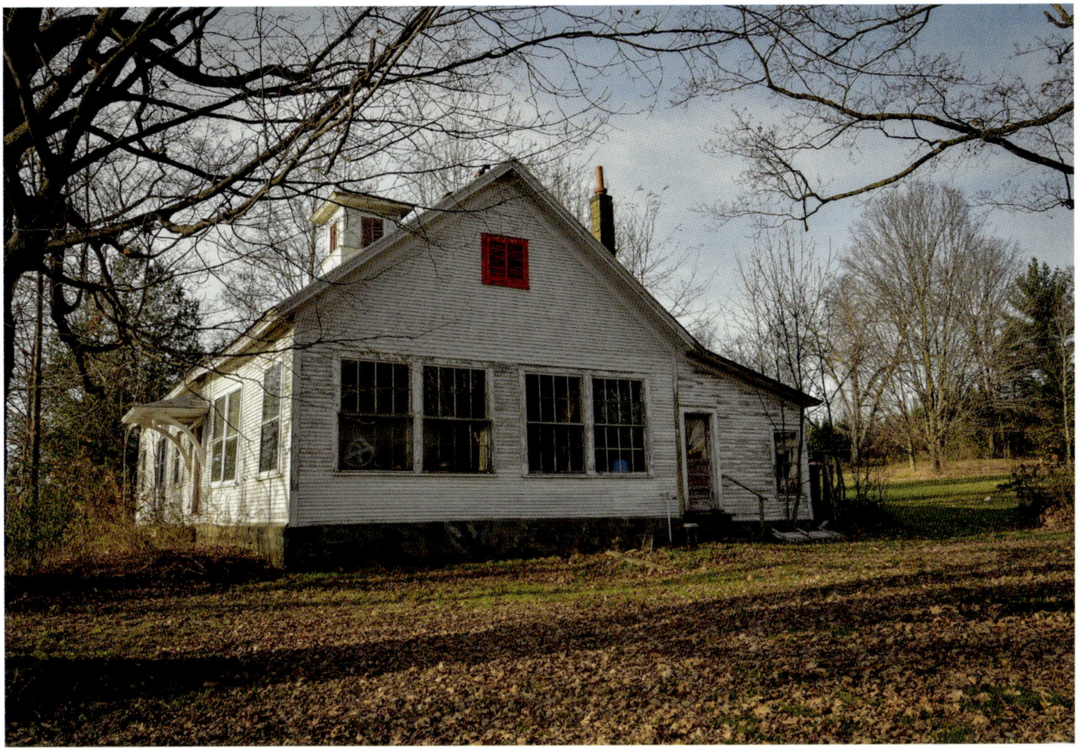

From the looks of this structure, it appears to be another abandoned schoolhouse.

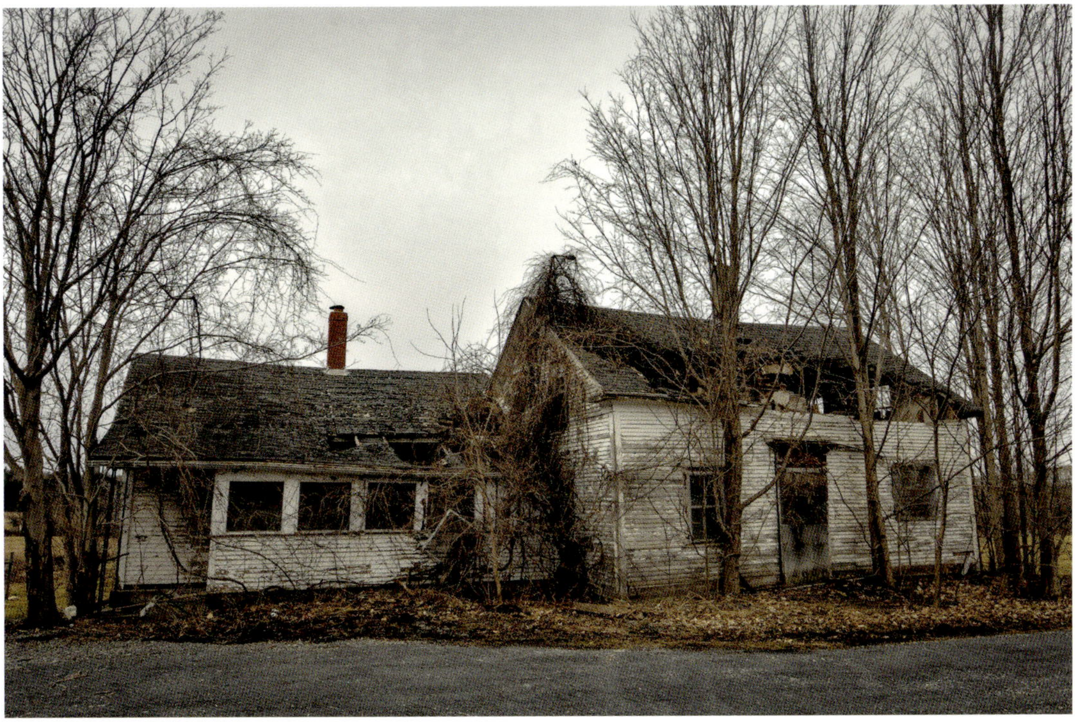

This spooky looking house has seen better days.

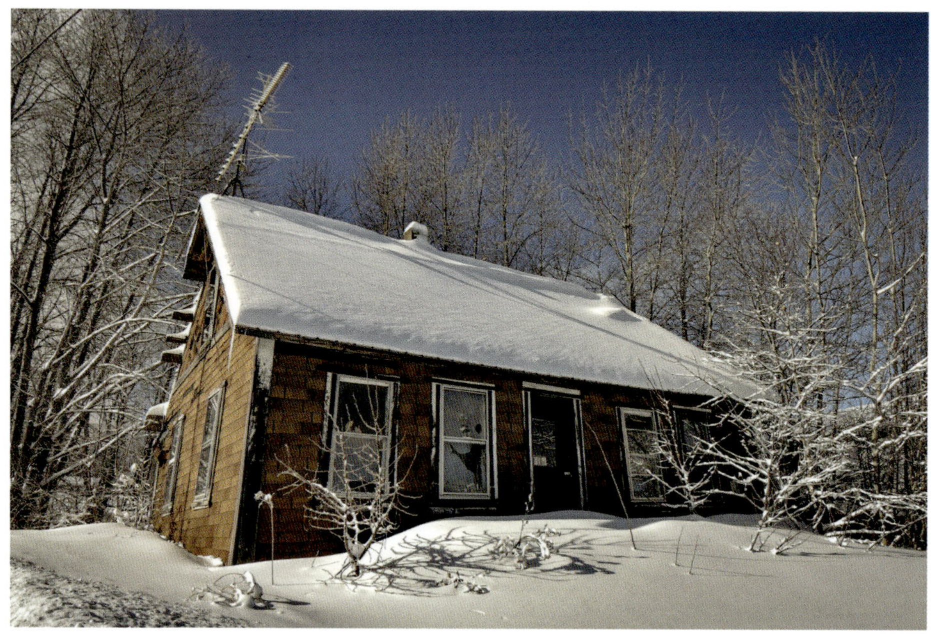

Another long, cold Vermont winter.

There was no shortage of family to make memories with, especially considering the matriarch of the family, Simmone, was one of fifteen children herself. Like with many large families, their door was always open, and the food was always on the table, offering a warm welcome to anyone who stopped by to make memories of their own.

New Hampshire is home to the raw material that is used for making whetstones. Due to this, an industry was created and quite a few factories were built over the years.

One major factory was The Pike Company. Founded by Isaac Pike in the 1840s, The Pike Company grew, expanded, and became the largest producer of whetstones in the world. The company made a variety of stones for various industries. The Pike Company, on its path of continued growth, bought up the competition. And, by the 1890s, the company dominated the market.

The introduction of the railroad in 1853 changed things for the factory and for the small village as well. A local newspaper noted that by 1901, the little village was home to 500 people and consisted of the whetstone mill, a sawmill, a hotel, stables, a schoolhouse, a post office, boarding houses, and several stores.

Driving down the road through the village now, it's clear all of that is a distant memory. All that is left of the once busy factory village is a single smokestack and small brick building.

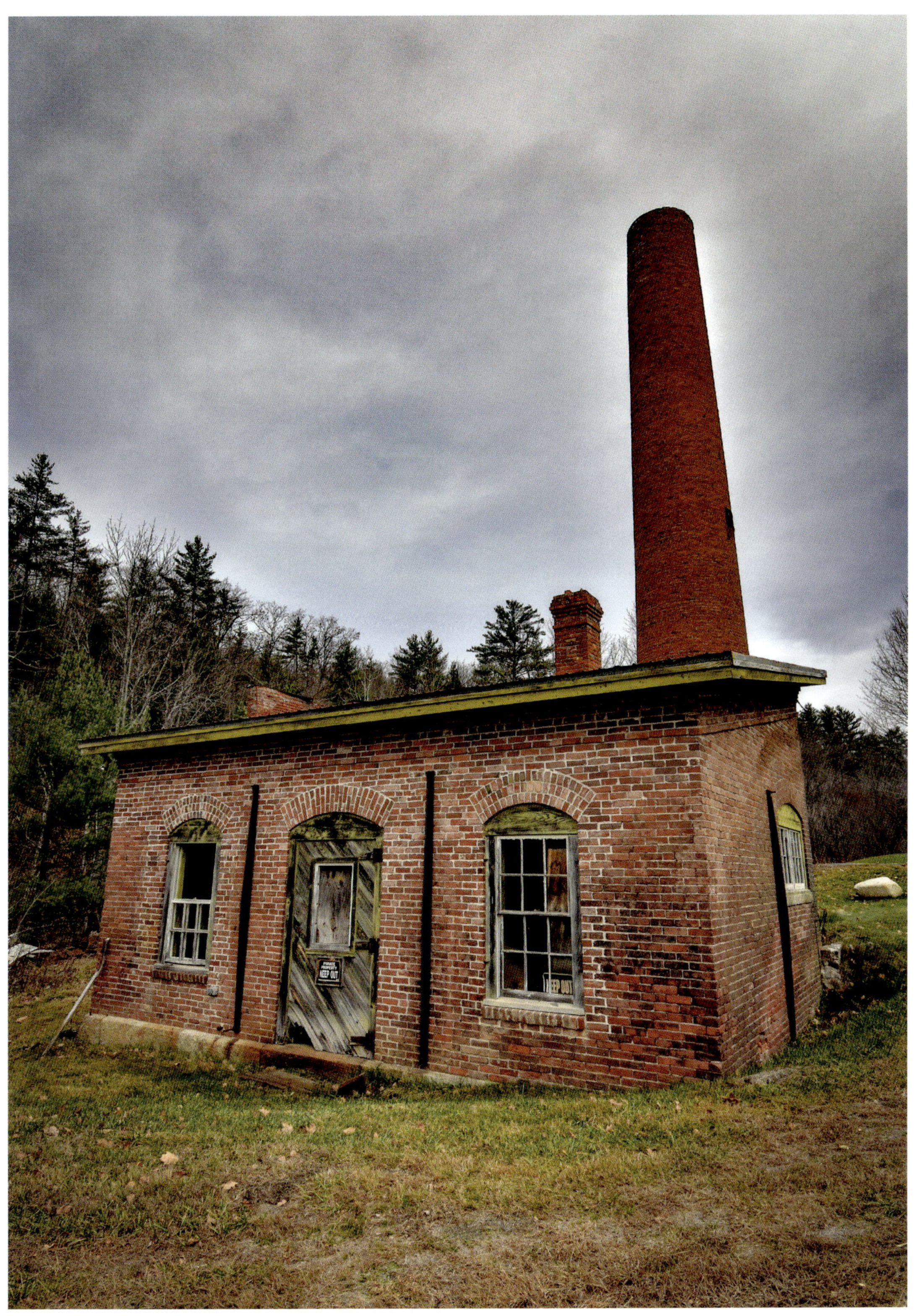

The smokestack is all that's left of the village.

Since elementary school, I always said that I would one day buy my grandparents' house. On the day that I did, unlocking the same door and turning the doorknob I had turned thousands of times before, just felt different. I had turned thirty just two weeks prior to signing my name and making my childhood dream come true, and this felt like a much-needed accomplishment after a long string of failures. The road to get to that point was filled with more downs than ups, but opening the door to my house, and my new life, truly made it all worth it to me. I had done something I was never sure I would. So many of my greatest and worst moments existed behind that doorknob. I lived there with my mother and grandparents when I was a baby, before my mom met the man who chose to be my dad. I shared countless laughs there with my brother and cousins. I lived there for a little while with my grandma after my grandpa passed away, and we spent nights eating ice cream and watching *The Golden Girls*. I was engaged, married, and divorced there. I adopted and brought home Sukha, my forever copilot there. I cried myself to sleep there after my nana and my grandma passed away. I sat up at night, questioning failed relationships there. I stressed out about layoffs and starting new jobs there. And, toward the end, for a little while, I got to share it with the person who means the most to me. He got to see how important that place was to me and how it was the keeper of most of my best and worst moments, and such a large piece of my history. And he shared my sadness when I decided it was time to move on from there. But every moment there, good or bad, started with turning the doorknob. Through the years, we were all a part of that house's history as well, and now it has different people creating a new chapter in its life story.

How many people closed the doors of these now abandoned places, not realizing that it was going to be the last time? And if they did know that it would be the last, how much time was spent thinking about the history shared between them before the door was finally locked? I always try to remain hopeful that these places will find someone to give them a new chapter to add to their stories, and that they aren't destined to be forgotten forever.

And for the forgotten places in this book that will never get that second chance, these pages are for you.

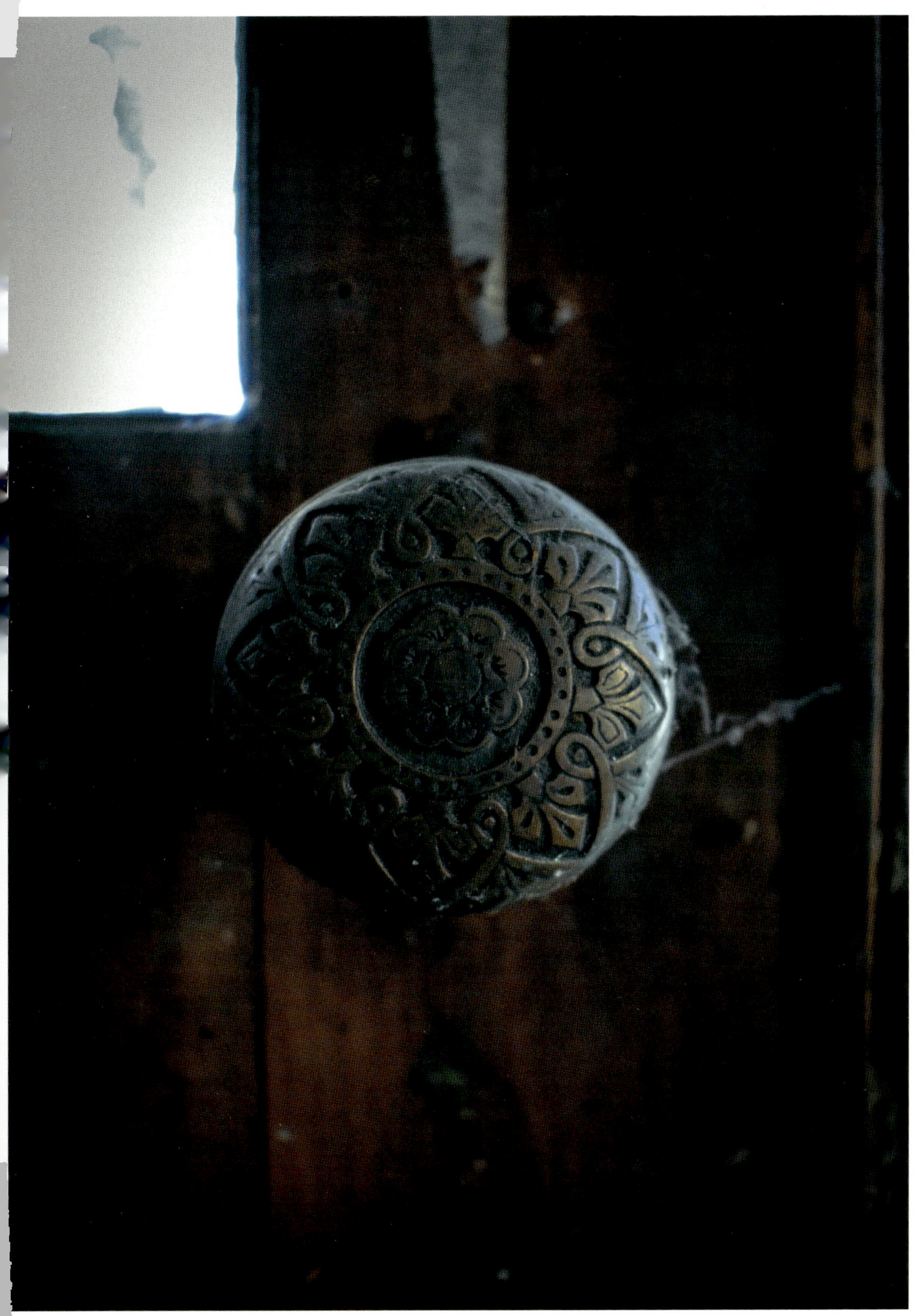

Ornate doorknob.

RESOURCES

Bethlehem Historical Society
Jefferson Historical Society
pittsburg-nh.com/index.php/about-pittsburg/town-history/41-indian-stream-republic
vermonter.com/curse-of-brunswick-springs
whitemountainhistory.org/Pike_New_Hampshire.html

Special Thanks

Katie Leclerc, Giacomo "Jack" Iozzo's grandniece, for sharing his story with me. Pamela Fournier Carley for sharing her fond memories of Cotter farm, which belonged to her aunt, uncle, and many cousins.